W9-ANY-334

FLORIDA STATE
UNIVERSITY LIBRARIES

JUN 1 1999

TALLAHASSEE, FLORIDA

OUR CONTINENT,
OUR FUTURE

OUR CONTINENT, OUR FUTURE

African Perspectives on Structural Adjustment

Thandika Mkandawire
& Charles C. Soludo

COUNCIL FOR THE DEVELOPMENT OF
SOCIAL SCIENCE RESEARCH IN AFRICA

Africa World Press, Inc.

P.O. Box 1892
Trenton, NJ 08607

P.O. Box 48
Asmara, ERITREA

INTERNATIONAL DEVELOPMENT RESEARCH CENTRE
Ottawa • Cairo • Dakar • Johannesburg • Montevideo • Nairobi • New Delhi • Singapore

HC
800
.M57
1999

© Council for the Development of Social Science Research in Africa 1999

All rights reserved. No part of this publication may be reproduced, stored in a retrieval system, or transmitted, in any form or by any means, electronic, mechanical, photocopying, or otherwise, without the prior permission of the publishers.

COUNCIL FOR THE DEVELOPMENT OF
SOCIAL SCIENCE RESEARCH IN AFRICA
Avenue Cheikh Anta Diop, Angle Canal IV, BP 3304 Dakar, Senegal
ISBN 2-86978-074-5

CODESRIA would like to express its gratitude to the Swedish Development Co-operation Agency (SIDA/SAREC), the Rockefeller Foundation, the International Development Research Centre (IDRC), the Ford Foundation, the Carnegie Corporation, the European Union, the Norwegian Ministry of Foreign Affairs, the Danish Agency for International Development (DANIDA), the Dutch Government, and the Government of Senegal for support of its research and publication activities.

INTERNATIONAL DEVELOPMENT RESEARCH CENTRE
PO Box 8500, Ottawa, ON, Canada K1G 3H9

Canadian Cataloguing in Publication Data
Mkandawire, P. Thandika
Our continent, our future : African perspectives on structural adjustment
Includes bibliographical references and index.
ISBN 0-88936-855-4
1. Structural adjustment (Economic policy) — Africa.
2. Africa — Economic conditions — 1960– .
3. Africa — Economic policy.
4. Africa — Social conditions — 1960– .
I. Soludo, Charles Chukwuma.
II. International Development Research Centre (Canada).
III. Title.
HC800.M55 1998   338.96   C98-901277-8

AFRICA WORLD PRESS, INC.
PO Box 1892, Trenton, NJ, USA / PO Box 48, Asmara, Eritrea

Library of Congress Cataloging in Publication Data
Mkandawire, P. Thandika
        Our continent, our future : African perspectives on structural
        adjustment / by Thandika Mkandawire & Charles C. Soludo.
                p. cm.
        Includes bibliographical references and index.
        ISBN 0-86543-704-1 (hb). --ISBN 0-86543-705-X (pb).
        1. Structural adjustment (Economic policy) -- Africa. 2. Africa -
- Economic conditions--1960– 3. Africa -- Economic policy. 4. Africa -
-Social conditions--1960– I. Soludo, Charles Chukwuma. II. Title.
HC800.M57   1998
338.96--dc21   98-41439
                                                         CIP

Contents

Foreword

Africa's dismal economic performance over the past 20 years has given rise to a number of attempts to explain and understand the causes of such performance. Growth regressions of various vintages identified a large, negative "African dummy" indicating that, indeed, African growth rates were far below those in other regions of the world. As well, most studies seem to confirm the importance of the core variables targeted under past adjustment programs: inflation rate, exchange rate, interest rate, and budget deficit. However, despite nearly two decades of reform, much of Africa remains impoverished.

A major irony of African development history is that the theories and models employed have largely come from outside the continent. No other region of the world has been so dominated by external ideas and models. A growing number of institutions and scholars have expressed serious concerns about this foreign domination, issuing a clarion call for Africans to lead in the reform process and to think for themselves. This major challenge is answered by this book.

Our Continent, Our Future presents an attempt by a number of African scholars to regain the initiative in matters relating to the future development of Africa. It presents an African perspective on the accumulated evidence about Africa's poor economic performance and is in keeping with the recent call by the Chief Economist to the World Bank, J. Stiglitz, for a search for wider goals and more instruments in a move beyond the Washington Consensus.

A simple, straightforward, and correct reading of the accumulated evidence clearly shows that first-generation, or orthodox, adjustment programs did not answer Africa's fundamental development questions. Evidence also demonstrates development work must transcend narrow concerns of macroeconomic stabilization. African policymakers and scholars have consistently called for a broadening of the objectives of development to include sustainability, equity, and governance. It is perhaps comforting that this call is now being widely heard and accepted.

Thandika Mkandawire and Charles Soludo, two of Africa's top scholars, have been active participants for many years in the debates on adjustment in Africa. In this book, they provide a succinct, yet comprehensive synthesis of the adjustment debate from a truly African perspective. They urge Africans to re-enter the debate and to take control in charting their socioeconomic and development future. In light of the recent economic crisis in Asia, where development success was hitherto proclaimed, this call is all the more pertinent and timely.

History and experience have taught us that development is a complex process and that no one has all the answers. At the turn of the millennium, Africans must take a long and hard look at their development problematique because, in the end, only Africans can develop Africa. This book provides important input in the search for a new consensus on Africa's development agenda in the 21st century. I strongly recommend it to policymakers, analysts, researchers, academics, and development professionals around the world.

K.Y. Amoaka
Executive Secretary
Economic Commission for Africa
Addis Ababa, Ethiopia

Acknowledgments

In writing this synthesis volume, we have drawn extensively from some of the papers prepared under the case studies. The very stimulating discussions and debates during the two workshops on this project also influenced some of the arguments here. We thank members of the steering committee (Ali A.G. Ali; E. Inanga; A. Oyejide; G. Ssemogerere; T. Tshibaka; S. Wangwe) for their overall guidance. In particular, we thank Dr Osita Ogbu for his comments and tireless insistence on excellence and the "Africanness" of the viewpoints, as well as Professors Ali Ali and Eno Inanga for their insightful comments and suggestions on an earlier draft. Madame Ngone Tine provided able research assistance for the project, and the Council for the Development of Social Science Research in Africa — the host institution — provided excellent support and coordination. The African Economic Research Consortium (AERC) also gave logistical assistance during one of the meetings of the Steering Committee, and we benefited from contacts with researchers from AERC during one of its annual meetings. We also thank the Centre for Development Research, in Copenhagen, for its hospitality during the final writing of the document.

Finally, we thank the International Development Research Centre, the Swedish International Development Authority, the Swedish Agency for Research Cooperation with Developing Countries, and the Dutch Ministry of Foreign Affairs for their financial assistance.

In addition to the Steering Committee, we thank the following, who were project participants: S. Adejumobi, M. Ayogu, B. Bouabré, G. Daffé, A. Diagne, C. Dordunoo, O. Eghosa, D. Ekpenyong, C. Emenuga, C. Ewonkem, N. Hussain, C.V Izeogu, M. Jama, T.L. Kasongo, E.W.E. Khidir, O. Kouassy, N.A. Lumumba, R. Meena, H.P.B. Moshi, F. Mwega, F. Ogwumike, A. Olukoshi, T. Oshikoya, A. Salau, and H.H. Semboja.

Introduction

For almost two decades, countries in sub-Saharan Africa (SSA) have implemented structural-adjustment programs (SAPs), and at the threshold of a new millennium, Africa may be graduating from being a region with "lost development decades" to becoming the world's "forgotten continent." After more than a decade of acrimonious debates and tonnes of evaluation reports, there is an increasing convergence of views that SAPs have not worked and that, as designed, they are grossly defective as a policy package for addressing the endemic poverty and pervasive underdevelopment of the region. In *Adjustment in Africa*, the World Bank (1994, p. 1) insisted, contrary to all evidence (including several of its own contradictory reports), that "adjustment is working." More recently, however, such self-assurances of the past seem to be giving way to a subdued humility, expressed in such phrases as "development everywhere is a complex phenomenon," "nobody has all the answers," "learning from experience," and "rapidly changing realities." This recent "rethinking" and admission that the Bretton Woods institutions (BWIs) do not have all the answers signal an imperative for Africans to devise strategies for the future of their countries. One also hopes that others can be persuaded to be more open minded in "policy dialogues" with their African counterparts.

On their part, African scholars and policymakers have been largely critical of the SAPs in their disparate writings on the subject. A careful reading of the writings of these African scholars indicates a discernible trend in terms of an emerging perspective. The need to sift through diverse perspectives in a single volume as a way of initiating and advancing continued dialogue on the issues provided the prime motivation for this project. Furthermore, throughout the adjustment years, the BWIs seized much of the initiative and foreclosed the debate by literally insisting that it was either their way or nothing, and African scholars were largely forced to assume reactive positions. Orthodox explanations of the African crisis have been based on a cognitive model of African elites, economies, and societies that has produced a view that is often paternalistic and contemptuous of local initiatives. It is a view that, in many ways, denies the Africans the capacity to learn from others or to implement the simplest of policies. How else can one read the following statement by the World Bank (1994, p. 194) on the lessons African countries can draw from the Asian experience?

> Because most countries are small, the market segments they succeed in will be narrow. That makes it unlikely that government (or internal agencies) can identify those segments in advance. Governments can help entrepreneurs discover and develop competitive exports by getting out of the way.

A dominant view among African scholars is that Africans should reenter the debate and assume the leading role in defining the continent's development agenda. The increasing need to think ourselves out of the crisis demands that we build on the lessons learned so far under the SAPs. With such an objective, about 30 studies (largely determined by the authors through their research proposals) were commissioned. About 25 of these were undertaken by economists, making this project the one with the largest participation of African economists on the issue of adjustment and the way forward (see the list of participants in the research network given in the Acknowledgments). Each of the studies appraises the performance of SAPs with respect to particular sectors or issues and evaluates the compatibility of the policies with the requirements for long-term development. Participants in the project set out to analyze the various policies under the SAPs from the perspective of development — broadly understood as involving economic growth, structural change, and elimination of poverty. The results of the studies were presented at two research workshops in Abidjan. One common conclusion in all the reports is that adjustment has not worked as promised. Each paper concludes with a number of recommendations pertaining to the way forward.

It is evident from the studies that a certain perspective is emerging among African scholars about what the SAPs can and cannot do and about the imperatives of a sound policy framework to address the fundamental crises of the region — poverty and underdevelopment. The synthesis of these studies and their common perspective is the focus of this volume, and the collection of selected papers will be published in a case-studies volume. The synthesis draws liberally from the individual studies, as well as from the authors' own reading, writing, and thinking on the subject. However, it does not provide a policy blueprint for each and every African country. What we have sought to emphasize is the need to make policy design sensitive to each individual country's historical and initial conditions.

We have also argued for a broader policy agenda for African countries and for a much more active role for the state within what is largely a market economy. The policy context is that of a mixed economy, in which the state and market are mutually supportive, in contrast to the one-sided "market-friendliness" of orthodox injunctions. We stress the role of the state in the development process, which has unfortunately been denigrated by a jaundiced view of the African state, with the result that African states are counseled to be least useful at precisely the moment when their societies need them most. Neither the vivid accounts of the people's heroic and ingenious methods of survival outside the ambit of failed states nor the egregious mismanagement of public affairs by many African leaders obviates the need for the state in the process of development. Constructing a state devoted to the public interest, including economic- and social-development forces, is not a technical process but a political process determined by each country's history, configuration of consensus on the key social parameters, and objectives.

We have devoted considerable space to recounting postcolonial history and the context of policy-making. We have recounted the "internalist" and "externalist" dichotomy of causes of the crisis. In debates on policy in Africa, emphasis on either the external or the internal factors has taken the form of allocating blame. We do not necessarily wish to resolve this debate. Our understanding is that, if policy is to make sense, it is important to have as precise a knowledge as possible of the objective conditions, both internal and external, that determine the context. Moreover, even if the external factors were "to blame," it will primarily be the responsibility of Africans to devise policies to reduce the vulnerability of their economies to such exogenous factors. If the factors are internal, it is again the Africans who will have to devise and implement the necessary policy changes. This is particularly true in the highly unlikely event that others will so adjust the external environment as to facilitate Africa's economic policies or will have the wisdom and competence to introduce, on our behalf, policies that will make our economies develop.

We stress that Africa must, and can, compete in an increasingly globalized world. Acquiring such a competitive capacity is not facilitated by the state simply "getting out of the way" as the World Bank counsels (World Bank 1994). This is not a passive process of simply reducing state intervention and relying on "market forces" but involves risk-taking and decisions about what sectors are potentially likely to yield long-term comparative advantages for African countries, modes of financing change, the nature and incidence of sacrifices to be borne, and so on. It also involves risk of error in a global context of extreme uncertainty. An open, transparent, and democratic process of consultation and debate over policy, facilitated by local technical competence, is central to such decisions.

In Chapter 1, we broadly describe the initial conditions of the African economies before the economic crisis. In Chapter 2, we critically examine the orthodox diagnosis of the causes of the crisis and key aspects of the policy prescriptions. Although our interpretation is not intended to defend policy mistakes of the past, it is designed to put the analysis of the crisis in perspective, especially given the warped diagnosis of orthodox analysis. Chapter 3 analyzes the results of adjustment experience in Africa, and Chapter 4 articulates the way forward by summarizing what appears to be the emerging African perspective on structural adjustment.

Chapter 1

BACKGROUND
Assessing Initial Conditions

Economists have generally identified "path dependence" as one of the important features of the growth process — that is, what eventually happens to an economy depends greatly on the point of departure. There is mounting evidence that large qualitative differences in outcomes can arise from small (and perhaps accidental) differences in initial conditions or events (Hurwicz 1995). In other words, the scope for and the direction and magnitude of change that a society can undertake depend critically on its prevailing objective conditions and the constellation of sociopolitical and institutional factors that have shaped these conditions.

For specific economies, the initial conditions affecting economic growth include levels of per capita income; the development of human capital; the natural-resource base; the levels and structure of production; the degree of the economy's openness and its form of integration into the world system; the development of physical infrastructure; and institutional variables such as governance, land tenure, and property rights. One might add here the nature of colonial rule and the institutional arrangements it bequeathed the former colonies, the decolonization process, and the economic interests and policies of the erstwhile colonial masters.

Wrongly specifying these initial conditions can undermine policy initiatives. Government polices are not simply a matter of choice made without historical or socioeconomic preconditions. Further, a sensitive appreciation of the differences and similarities in the initial conditions is important if one is to avoid some of the invidious comparisons one runs into today and the naive voluntarism that policymakers exhibit when they declare that their particular countries are about to become the "New Tigers" of Africa. Such mindless comparisons and self-description actually make the process of learning from others more costly because they start the learning process off on a wrong foot.

The Bretton Woods institutions (BWIs) have held two not always mutually compatible positions on the initial conditions of African economies. At times, they have pointed to how initial conditions in a number of African countries were the same as or even better than those in the subsequently more successful Asian cases. At other times, they have argued, in a "back-to-the future" mode of thinking, that because the conditions in Africa today are comparable to those of the Asian economies more than 30 years ago, Africa is now ready for an Asian-type takeoff.

Although cross-regional or cross-country comparisons are inevitable in economic analysis, choosing the "right" countries, periods, and appropriate statistics to compare is often problematic. A comparison between two countries or regions based on a snapshot of conditions at a particular time can be grossly misleading. For example, although the Russian Federation can be compared in terms of per capita income to many developing countries, its stock of scientific and technological capability can hardly be compared with that of any developing country. Such differences in the quality of labour force and stock of knowledge can make monumental differences in the acceleration of the growth process. An alternative (sometimes complementary) comparison is between countries' current and past performance or initial conditions. We emphasize more the latter and also employ cross-regional comparisons where relevant.

In this chapter, we have devoted considerable space to recounting postcolonial economic history, objective conditions, and context of policymaking. This provides a context for a meaningful diagnosis of the African crisis. The analysis of the initial conditions emphasizes mainly the precrisis period — from independence in the early 1960s through the late 1970s.

Physical conditions

Africa is a vast continent with enormous ecological variation. A home of some of the world's major rain forests, it is also the home of arid and semi-arid spaces that suffer severe climatic changes with an almost biblical regularity. One positive side of such diversity is that it can support a diversified agricultural base and intracontinental trade. It does, however, create a great need for location-specific research.

Africa has the largest concentration of landlocked countries in the world. Given the overall poor infrastructure and the colonial patterns of communication linkages, this geographical situation compounds the problems of development for many countries. It not only adds to the high transport cost but also places key aspects of a country's policies in the hands of coastal neighbours. Crises in the neighbouring countries can impose heavy financial transaction costs on trade, as shown by the price paid by Malawi and Zimbabwe after the civil war in Mozambique. Even more critically, the geographical situation raises the level of uncertainty about investing in specific African countries.

At least when compared with Asia, Africa is still largely a continent with a "land surplus." Its relative thinness of population over vast distances is made even thinner by the extremely poor development of physical infrastructure. Killick (1995) cited a study by Ahmed and Rustagi (1987) that showed that in 1976, 11 countries of sub-Saharan Africa (SSA) had a mean road density of 0.05 km/km^2, compared with 0.35, 0.41, and 0.41 km/km^2 for Bangladesh, India, and Indonesia. The study also showed that these three countries had an average of 36% of their roads paved, against a mean for the SSA countries of 14%. The deterioration of infrastructure since then has most probably widened the gap between African and Asian countries.

In most recent attempts to explain Africa's performance with growth and investment regressions, studies find that inaccessible location, poor port facilities, and the "Dutch Disease" syndrome, caused by large natural-resource endowments, constitute serious impediments to investment and growth. Sachs and Warner (1996), for instance, estimated that these factors account for about 1.2% per annum deterioration in growth. In an earlier study, Sachs and Warner (1995) demonstrated that large natural-resource endowments tend to retard growth because of the loss of externalities as a result of the smaller size of the remaining tradable-goods sector. Although legitimate arguments can be made about the size of the negative effects of the natural and physical characteristics, these studies emphasize the peculiar disadvantages faced by Africa because of these features.

Human capital

Africa has extremely low levels of human-capital formation, as measured by levels of literacy and school enrolment. A remarkable outcome of colonial rule in Africa, especially when compared with Japanese colonial rule in Korea and even American colonial rule in the Philippines, is the extremely low level of social development in terms of health and education indicators.

Figure 1. Per capita income in sub-Saharan Africa, 1962–94.

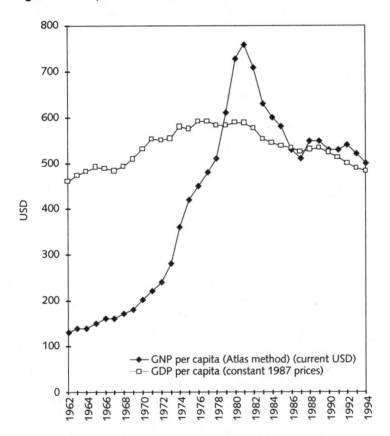

Source: Calculated from World Bank data disks.
Note: GDP, gross domestic product; GNP, gross national product; USD, United States dollars.

In several social indicators — life expectancy, secondary-school enrolment, infant mortality, and population per physician — Africa has only in the 1990s reached the corresponding Asian levels. SSA in 1990 was, however, still far worse off than Asia was in 1965 with respect to primary-school enrolment and adult illiteracy, which were 68% and 50% in SSA but 80% and 35% in Asia. In terms of growth rates, Africa has had the most spectacular performance in the area of education (relative to the state at independence), but one cannot deny that SSA was, and remains, the region with the highest illiteracy rates and least access to basic health and social services.

Economic performance

An understanding of the adjustment experience in Africa requires a brief historical account of the preadjustment years. This is for a number of reasons. First, it is important to dispel the idea that the decline of African economies is an almost ineluctable postcolonial syndrome inherent to African political and societal forces and, therefore, policy-making. Such a view, initially given credence by the World Bank's Berg report (World Bank 1981), is widely held among North American political scientists who have invested considerable amounts of research explaining what in fact never happened, that is, that ever since independence, African economies have been on the decline. Second, it is important to recall this experience not only because of the path dependence of economies but also because it can help us identify the potential sources of growth and indicate the sustainability of such patterns of growth if they are to be revived today, as suggested by those who propose back-to-the-future scenarios for Africa. Third, the history of the preadjustment years can show us what gains have been made, the fragility or robustness of such gains as bases for further advancements, the capacities that have been developed, and the lessons to be learned from Africa's own experiences, all of which can give us a better understanding of the task ahead. Finally, to the extent that the cost and speed of adjustment depend on the structure of the economy and its social capacity to adjust, developed over many years before adjustment, we must understand the degree of flexibility or inflexibility an economy has acquired. "Good policies" introduced in complete ignorance of such conditions inevitably fail and may even make things worse.

Postcolonial African economic history is one of fairly respectable rates of growth for nearly a decade (including some "miracles" in a number of countries) and then a decline after the oil crisis of the mid-1970s.

Between 1965 and 1974, annual growth in gross domestic product (GDP) per capita averaged 2.6%. From 1974 on, it stagnated; by the end of the 1980s, many African countries had a lower GDP per capita than at independence. This inverted-V pattern, with the apex over the mid-1970s, is true of virtually every economic indicator except agricultural output. Changes in GDP per capita and changes in gross national product (GNP), determined with the World Bank "Atlas" method, clearly show an increase in per capita income up to 1980 or so and a decline since then (Figure 1). Yet the Berg report (World Bank 1981) was essentially premised on postcolonial decline, even while conceding, rather grudgingly, that African economies had witnessed per capita increases in the postcolonial era.

A better picture of the relative and absolute deterioration in Africa's performance since the 1980s is clear from Table 1. Although never spectacular by the standards of other developing regions, the growth in SSA countries was modest (Tables 1 and 2) in the two decades after independence and showed persistent deterioration thereafter, even in relation to past performances of these countries. Comparisons with the rest of the world, especially other developing countries, also emphasize the poor performance of the region. Aggregating all countries and taking decade averages, however, conceals individual-country differences, year-to-year variations, and per capita income performance. On the whole, economic performance (as measured by GDP per capita) has been poor and worsening, especially since the late 1970s. As Collier and Gunning (1997) observed,

Table 1. Average annual growth in per capita GDP in regions and countries of the world, 1960–91.

	Average annual growth (%)			
	1960–69	1970–79	1980–91	1960–91
Sub-Saharan Africa	1.2	1.6	–0.6	0.6
Developing countries	1.9	2.3	0.0	1.3
Latin America and the Caribbean	2.2	2.3	–0.8	1.0
North Africa, Middle East, and Asia	2.9	4.0	2.3	2.8
Countries of the OECD	4.2	2.6	1.6	2.7
World	2.4	2.4	0.3	1.6

Source: Nissanke (1997).
Note: GDP, gross domestic product; OECD, Organisation for Economic Co-operation and Development.

GDP per capita declined by 1.3% per annum during the 1980s, a full 5 percentage points below the average for all low-income developing countries. This deterioration was even worse during 1990–94, at 1.8% per annum, further widening the gap with other developing countries to 6.2 percentage points. Evidently, despite the reforms, SSA is still years away from recovering the modest performance of the postindependence era.

These facts lead to the important observation that African countries have not only performed much worse than their Asian counterparts during the last decade and a half but also performed much worse than they had previously — a performance that must be recalled if Africa is not to be condemned to the ridiculously low measures of "success" that are now peddled by international financial institutions so desperate for evidence of the usefulness of their prescriptions. This said, previous good performance must be examined critically because even if it can be replicated today, it might have characteristics that would make it unsustainable. Indeed, to understand the deterioration in performance, it is important to shed some light on the dynamic characteristics that made the "good performance" of the postindependence era unsustainable.

Table 2. Africa's economic performance, 1965–94.

Indicator	Performance (%)				
	1965–73	1974–79	1980–85	1986–93	1990–94
Population growth rate	2.7	2.9	3.0	3.0	3.0
Growth rate of GDP (avg)	5.7	3.5	1.8	2.5	1.9
Growth rate of per capita GDP (avg)	3.0	0.7	–1.1	–0.5	–1.1
Growth rate of agricultural output (avg)	2.7	3.0	1.5	2.7	2.1
Growth rate of manufacturing output (avg)	7.3	6.7	5.2	2.5	1.3
Investment–GDP (avg)	16.5	20.9	16.3	15.6	15.3
Growth rate of investment (avg)	9.6	6.9	–4.8	1.2	0.8
Savings–GDP (avg)	16.2	19.7	14.9	13.8	12.7
Growth rate of exports (avg)	8.2	2.6	0.4	3.0	0.6
Growth rate of imports (avg)	7.4	6.2	–2.4	0.7	0.4
Fiscal balance–GDP	NA	–5.4	–9.0	–8.7	–4.8
Resource balance	1.0[a]	–3.6[b]	–2.8	–3.5[c]	–1.6
Rate of inflation (avg)	5.8	13.8	18.8	21.7	27.2

Source: ADB (1994).
Note: Avg, average; GDP, gross domestic product; NA, not available.
[a]1965.
[b]1975–79.
[c]1986–90.

Characteristic features

Several features of the "precrisis" performance need to be examined because they point both to Africa's great potential and to the inherent limitations of the policies pursued in the period before the structural-adjustment programs (SAPs). They also point to the fact that any adjustment strategy that fails to address these issues is far from adequate and may at best merely reproduce the flawed "good performance" of the past.

EXTREME DEPENDENCE ON EXTERNAL CONDITIONS

One of the notable initial conditions of SSA economies is the atypically high dependence of economic performance on the external environment. Three aspects of the external environment (that is, outside the control of policymakers) are

- The trade-related factors (terms of trade and volatility of markets for Africa's exports);
- The climatic conditions (mainly drought); and
- The prevalence of civil strife and wars in the continent.

Most African countries have preserved a major legacy of colonialism, that is, concentration of export earnings on one or few primary commodities that are highly vulnerable to exogenous terms of trade and demand conditions. African economies depend heavily on this primary, often enclave, sector for foreign-exchange earnings and government revenue. It is, therefore, not surprising that an often-cited study (Wheeler 1994) found an extremely close relationship between movements in export prices and average economic performance through the precrisis, postindependence era. The relatively good economic performance took place during the "Golden Era of Capitalism," when the buoyant economies of the developed countries provided ever-expanding markets for Africa's primary produce. Collier and Gunning (1997) stressed that since 1980, which is the period during which African decline has been most pronounced, the terms of trade have deteriorated more on most measures in Africa than in other regions.

Even if the terms of trade had not deteriorated more in Africa than elsewhere, the peculiarly feeble production structures and excessive dependence of the economy on a few products would have resulted in any negative shock having disproportionately damaging effects on Africa. The Wheeler (1994) study included the following explanatory variables: policy variables (effective exchange rate, an indicator of import-allocation practices, and a measure of the ability to preserve balance in trade accounts) and exogenous factors (rainfall, violence, terms of trade, foreign aid, remittances from migrant workers, stability in export earnings, and export diversification). The exogenous variables as a group enjoyed a dominant place. In more recent years, as adjustment has failed to yield the expected results, other studies have come to pretty much the same conclusion. It is important to remember this dependence on external factors for African economic successes and trials because until Africa's export is significantly diversified and anchored on a firm and better-articulated production base, external factors will continue to play a destabilizing role.

The exogenous conditions that dealt severe blows to many African economies were the droughts of 1973/74 and 1984/85, as well as the increase in civil disturbances in many countries. These conflicts, manifested in protracted civil wars, riots, and social unrest, created the largest refugee crisis in the world. The conflict spilt over into neighbouring countries not only in the form of refugees but also in the form of disruption of trade links and infrastructure and the worsening of Africa's image. The crisis accentuated the environment of uncertainty and directed the energies of many African states to a primary task of survival and maintenance of law and order, rather than priorities of longer-term development. Even outsiders who sought solidarity with Africa found themselves tying an increasing share of their aid to humanitarian activities. Meaningful economic development cannot take place without peace.

LOW INVESTMENT AND SAVINGS

Although the new growth theories remind us of the numerous determinants of economic growth other than physical capital, investment in such capital is still one of the most robust determinants of economic growth, and trends in the share of investment tell much of the African story and explain much of the continent's relative decline. Between 1965 and 1980, levels of investment in Africa increased and compared favourably to those of other developing regions, especially those without central planning. It is important to note that, up to 1975, much of the investment was financed with domestic savings; thus, savings and investment during the period were relatively highly correlated (Figure 2). This domestic capacity to finance relatively high levels of investments, at least when seen from the current vantage point, should be remembered as African countries consider the mobilization of resources for future development.

Two features of the investment process in postindependence Africa are worth noting. First, much of the private investment in the colonial

Figure 2. Gross domestic savings (GDS) and gross domestic investments (GDI) in Africa, 1960–93.

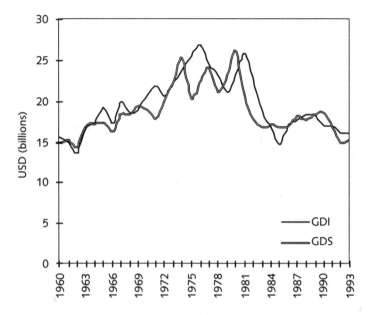

Source: Calculated from World Bank data disks.

period was dominated by foreigners. The domestic capitalist class was virtually absent in all but a handful of African countries. At the eve of independence, countries saw capital flight and deinvestment, perhaps owing to fear of the incoming nationalist governments. After independence, despite the battery of incentives introduced by African governments (cofinancing, protection, tax holidays, repressive labour laws, and so forth), private (foreign) investment was still restrained. It was partly the response to this restraint and the weakness and nascence of indigenous capitalists that pushed most African governments toward the much bemoaned "statist" option. Most African governments moved into production simply to fill in the investment gap. Few nationalizations in Africa occurred outside the mining sector, and many of the state-owned industries were set up by the new governments themselves. It is, therefore, not surprising that public investment played a major role in the growth of aggregate investment in Africa. Such public-sector investment grew quickly to meet the postindependence goals of socioeconomic transformation and diversification. Investment in public schools, roads, hospitals, and industries grew rapidly. After the major external shocks of the mid-1970s, such levels of investment were no longer sustainable. In some countries, investment collapsed altogether, whereas others managed to sustain the trend through massive borrowing from abroad; these countries accumulated external debt rapidly as the consequence.

One other feature of investment was the poor response of domestic capital. To be sure, in the early years, such capital did not constitute much. However, judging by the cited magnitudes of capital flight, it later constituted a substantial amount of potentially invertible surplus. It has been estimated that by 1990, 37% of Africa's wealth had flown outside the continent (Collier and Gunning 1997). It is, therefore, important to know what factors lay behind the poor response of domestic capital. One factor was the hostility of African governments to domestic capital, even as they courted foreign capital. African governments seemed to work on the assumption that although foreign capital has no political claims, domestic capital would be expected to assert such claims and, therefore, threaten the political positions of the ruling elite. And so, even in countries where official ideology was favourable to capitalism, indigenous capital remained suspect in the eyes of the political elite. Consequently, the potential African investors (many of whom had made their money through "rents" from, and corrupt practices in, government) logically chose to keep most of their wealth abroad in what could be described as a "flight to safety." This point about the enduring tensions and suspicion between business and the ruling elite, a relationship characterized more by rivalry than by partnership, should be borne in mind by those designing strategies to encourage indigenous entrepreneurs to invest in Africa.

FLAWED INDUSTRIALIZATION[1]

For nearly all countries of SSA, the 1960s and 1970s marked the first attempt at industrialization. African countries, except for South Africa and Zimbabwe (then known as Rhodesia), had missed out during the import-substituting industrialization (ISI) that took place in Latin America and India under the "natural protection" of the Great Depression and World War II. Mkandawire (1988) discussed how Africa's industrialization has been out of phase with global trends during much of this century. Not surprisingly, at independence, SSA was the least industrialized part of

---

[1]This section draws heavily on Wangwe and Semboja (1998).

the world. Even in the more-industrialized African countries, such as Kenya and Zambia, the share of industry in GDP fell below the "Chenery norms" — in other words, their rates of industrialization were less than would be predicted by their per capita income and size of population.

It is, perhaps, therefore not surprising that the nationalists placed so much emphasis on promoting industrialization, which was perceived as an integral part of the development agenda and was expected to facilitate the transformation of predominantly agricultural economies to modern industrial economies. The share of industry in the economy was expected to rise, generate opportunities for employment, raise levels of productivity, and raise the incomes and standards of living of the majority of the population. The dominant view then was that such an industrialization would be premised on industrial policy deliberately designed to diversify the production base, encourage investment, and facilitate the acquisition of new technologies.

Although the key instrument was import substitution, it should be noted that there was always the implicit or explicit quest for diversification of exports to abolish inherited monocultural export structures. Autarky was never the policy objective of any African government, and import substitution was never an end in itself. The general expectation was that industrialization (initially through import substitution) would bring about restructuring of the predominantly primary-export sector into a more diversified export sector in which exports of industrial products would increasingly play an important role. Conventional wisdom was, after all, that industrial exports were associated with dynamic products involving specialization and technological learning. One should also recall the widely held belief that the balance-of-payments problems were associated with deteriorating terms of trade. If industrial goods that were imported could be produced at home instead, this would dampen the effects of unfavourable terms of trade and in the long run actually improve them by steering the structure of exports away from goods whose terms of trade tended to secularly decline. The production of formerly imported goods was accompanied by imports of capital goods and intermediate inputs needed to maintain desired levels of capacity use. We can identify three implications of this phenomenon. First, the desired production levels could only be maintained if adequate levels of imported inputs were maintained. This implied that foreign-exchange earnings had to meet the requirements for imported inputs to keep industry operating at the desired levels. Second, the industrial investments and operations were not necessarily associated with strong linkages with the rest of the economy. Although technology in the form of capital goods was embedded in the imports, little effort was put into technological learning. Third, to the extent that imports consisted of inputs essential to production and investment, failure to acquire the necessary foreign exchange for the continued purchase of these inputs led to capacity underuse and economic decline.

With the high levels of effective protection in the domestic markets, the industrial sector became exclusively inward oriented, with neither incentives nor compulsions to move toward an export orientation. Many inefficient firms were able to reap high profits in the domestic market while operating at relatively low levels of capacity use. Under the circumstances, such firms saw no reason to take the risks inherent in the competitive export markets. Besides the minimal processing of local natural resources, only a few of the industrial activities promoted in this period have matured to become fully competitive. Value-added export-oriented activities that have driven many dynamic developing economies (such as those of the Southeast Asian countries) are conspicuously absent in SSA. Despite the low wages, only a few labour-intensive activities aimed at world markets have taken root in Africa. Linkages between local industries remain minimal and mostly superficial. The technological level of the existing industrial activities remains generally low.

What emerges from all this is that although the professed objective of industrialization was to diversify exports to include more goods of high income elasticity, ISI as implemented in much of Africa lacked any strategy to move progressively to a greater emphasis on exports or to gain access to technology. This lack of strategy for export competitiveness, rather than import substitution per se, was the central problem of African industrialization. What eventually penalized Africa was the naive expectation that industry would somehow transform itself to achieve export diversification without explicit measures to push industry in this direction.

We should, however, note that these attempts at industrialization were not entirely wasted. One can argue, as it has been argued for Latin America (although perhaps with less force), that it is a misleading simplification to say that the ISI policy has left nothing behind except outmoded industrial plants and rent-seeking entrepreneurs incapable of functioning in a competitive international environment. Some technological capabilities were acquired and human skills enhanced through numerous and widespread learning mechanisms, and some individual firms and industries have managed to modernize and upgrade themselves substantially. It is also worth noting that industries that are now venturing into export markets are not the new ones spawned by the SAPs but those built during the phase of import substitution. Even the newly privatized industries are tapping into the managerial and technical skills acquired during the phase of ISI. The misfortune of Africa has been that the new policies, driven by an ideological aversion to public ownership and a complete misreading of the origins of ISI, have thrown away the proverbial baby with the bath water.

POOR PERFORMANCE OF AGRICULTURE

Agriculture was the Achilles heel of postcolonial economic performance. Between 1961 and 1994, Africa was the only one of all the major developing regions that suffered a decline in per capita levels of food production. Much of this decline has been blamed on policies that favoured industry or urban development and penalized agriculture. These policies were reflected in unfavourable terms of trade, poor distribution networks in the countryside because of state monopolies, poor agricultural infrastructure, and so forth. Adjustment was supposed to reverse the decline, initially by "getting prices right" through liberalization of markets and devaluation of currencies to favour the tradable goods, which were largely agricultural.

One should note parenthetically that just as with the economy as a whole, agricultural performance was not uniformly poor across all countries or during the entire postindependence period. In fact, until 1970/71, the trend in per capita production was upward. Studies cited by Delgado (1996) showed that from 1965 to 1973, both labour and land productivity grew, with labour-productivity growth exceeding land-productivity growth. In all the subregion, total factor productivity grew in the 1960s by an average of 1.4% but began to stagnate in the early 1970s. This said, the performance of African agriculture even before the crises in the 1970s left much to be desired.

Although there has been widespread consensus that agriculture was neglected by the state policies, analysts disagree strongly about the character of that negligence and the political reasons for it. Consequently, there are disagreements about the remedies. As noted in the "pricist" approaches, removal of factors leading to price distortions was expected to lead to better incentives for agricultural producers. This, in turn, was expected to elicit enough response in supply to reverse the downward trend in per capita levels of agricultural production. Critics of this approach pointed to the evidence that aggregate supply responses in agriculture were too low to yield the kind of supply responses expected by the pricists. However, the critics confused official prices with the real prices paid by consumers and to producers. Parallel markets were so widespread in Africa that it was unlikely that liberalization would have produced a radically different set of relative prices. The question that this should have raised was, why, despite favourable prices (especially for food crops), was African food production so poor?

African governments were not merely predatory in their relationship to agriculture. A more accurate characterization of their policies would be to say they were ambivalent and at times outright contradictory. Side by side with extraction of surplus through the export taxes and monopsonistic behaviour of their marketing boards, African governments have transferred resources to rural areas through input and credit subsidies, social expenditure, infrastructure development, extension services, and so forth. States that depended on mineral rents for revenue simply did not need the surpluses from the countryside. Thus, although agriculture suffered from the Dutch Disease effects of mineral development or adverse terms of trade, it could also receive considerable allocations of resources from the mining sector. The allocation of such resources was often guided by redistributive concerns, which partly explains why they led to only low levels of production.

The ambivalence and contradictions of the state policies reflected many factors that are often obscured by the simplistic rent-seeking and urban-bias interpretations. These factors included spatial egalitarianism that inspired panterritorial pricing, patronal–clientalist linkages that placed rural interests on the national agenda, imperatives of national cohesion, developmental concerns about increased rural productivity, food subsidies for urban populations, and fiscal needs of the state.

At the end of the 1970s, African agriculture had made little progress in terms of using inputs such as irrigation, fertilizers, and farming equipment. Not much had been achieved by way of increasing the sector's responsiveness to market signals. With the overarching emphasis on industrialization, the lack of adequate attention paid to developing policy for the agricultural sector is probably a major explanation for the stagnation. We shall return to the explanations for poor performance in the next two chapters.

Social development

Africa has undergone dramatic social change since independence, and much of this change has continued despite economic stagnation. The continent has witnessed significant demographic transformations, including much higher levels of urbanization. Levels of literacy are now much higher than they were at independence. New social classes have emerged in the wake of the indigenization of the African civil service and incipient industrialization. Urban centres have become cauldrons of enormous cultural creativity, new conflict, and new alliances.

Considerable investment was made in the social sector, especially in education, to counter Africa's colonial heritage of being the most educationally backward region in the world. The result of these social investments was an impressive improvement in levels of education and literacy. Primary-school enrolments increased from 41% of the eligible population to 68% between 1965 and the mid-1980s. A cadre of professionals was produced to administer the postcolonial states. Despite these achievements, however, indices of health and education lagged behind those of other developing countries.

Furthermore, despite the enormous efforts made in education and the quite significant increases in enrolment at higher levels (Table 3), the number of students enrolled after almost two decades of efforts remains far below the figures of other developing countries. For some countries, development in the SAP period shows rates of expansion that are less than population growth, implying a deterioration in levels of enrolment relative to population.

Table 3. Higher-education enrolment in selected African countries, 1960–90.

	Total (thousands)					Average annual growth (%)		
	1960	1970	1980	1985	1990	1960–80	1980–85	1985–90
Côte d'Ivoire	0.3	4.4	19.6	20.5	24.2	23.2	0.8	3.4
Ethiopia	0.9	4.5	14.4	27.3	34.1	14.9	13.7	4.5
Ghana	1.5	5.4	15.5	17.0	19.0	12.4	1.9	2.2
Kenya	1.0	7.8	13	21.8	33.0	13.7	10.9	8.7
Senegal	1.4	5.0	13.6	13.4	19.0	10.4	–0.4	7.3
Sudan	4.0	14.3	28.8	37.4	75.0	10.4	5.4	15.0
Tanzania	–	2.0	4.1	4.9	5.3	–	3.5	1.6
Togo	–	0.9	4.8	5.5	8.0	–	3.0	7.8
Zimbabwe	0.3	5.0	8.3	30.8	49.4	18.1	29.9	9.9

Source: Calculated from World Bank (1988).

Table 4. Enrolment in higher education in Africa and in other parts of the world.

	Total enrolment	Natural sciences	Engineering	Medical sciences
Africa (avg)	89.18	13.36	9.30	7.00
South America (avg middle income)	147.96	74.55	230.86	151.73
Countries of OECD (avg)	2 392.51	214.19	369.25	260.73

Source: Brautigam (1996).
Note: Avg, average; OECD, Organisation for Economic Co-operation and Development.

Whatever the calculations, it is quite clear that Africa's social capacity for rapid industrial development, structural transformation, and technological absorption is not enhanced by the extremely low levels of development of technical and scientific personnel, and current levels of enrolment fall far short of what Africa needs (Table 4).

Social differentiation

One significant social change has been the increase in social differentiation among Africans, which the leveling effect of colonialism had held in check or muted. By the mid-1970s, a number of studies began to suggest that economic growth in postcolonial Africa had been accompanied by growing inequity. Nationalists who had pronounced their society "classless" soon found themselves at the head of societies in which class had become increasingly salient. Industry was highly concentrated in one or two urban conglomerations; so was modern infrastructure. Where region was coterminous with ethnicity, such an uneven development could only fan the flames of ethnic conflicts. Such inequity existed not only along class, ethnic, and regional lines but also along gender lines. Modern formal-sector employment continued to be a largely male domain. Although women remained the key producers in agriculture, social changes in agriculture, especially commoditization, tended to work against women. Extension services and purveyors of new technologies and inputs tended to focus on male producers, even though the farm-level decisions were in female hands.

Despite this growing social differentiation, a certain fluidity in (class or economic) interest articulation permitted more flexibility in policy-making than some current analyses allow. It also accounts for the confusion and contradictory directions of African policy-making that belies much of the reductionist reconstruction of African policy-making.

Overall political-economic structure

The political-economic structure is probably the most difficult part of the puzzle of Africa's economic rise and fall. Much has been said about class and interest formation in Africa. What is clear is that at the national level, state–society relationships were quite fluid at the beginning. Most of the social classes or interest groups to whom certain policies are usually attributed in the more deductive formulations of policy-making in Africa simply did not exist at independence and were spawned by the process that they are said to have initiated. It is true that once such groups emerged around certain economic activities, they tended to defend them strongly.

It is also important to note that for all their rhetoric and pronouncements of idiosyncratic versions of "socialism," African economies remained largely market economies with varying levels of controls and "distortions." Reading some descriptions of African economies, one would think one was dealing with centrally planned economies (of the East European type), with the state in full control of all markets. Such a view is hardly accurate. By ideological inclination, institutional inheritance, and class interest, no African leader — not even the "Afro–Marxist" ones — could be said to have pursued anything similar to the centrally planned economies that then actually existed. If certain markets were not working, this was not always because the state had "suppressed" them so that they could emerge with the end of state repression. It was often the case that such markets never developed, or if they developed, they were monopolized by some public or private entity.

One should not forget that official pronouncements of "comprehensive development plans" did not amount to the institutionalization of effective planning. The reach of the state was limited, earning it such epithets as the "overextended state," the "soft state," and the "lame leviathan." One consequence of all this was that liberalization has been much less disruptive in Africa than in the centrally planned economies, and the extensive existence of markets — formal and informal, or parallel — accounts for the fact that liberalization has had marginal effects on the emergence, resurgence, or efficiency of markets in much of Africa. It is not surprising that liberalization has not led to the turnarounds expected or to the catastrophes actually visiting the former Soviet Union.

The political transformations

If the nationalist movements that assumed power did so on the basis of essentially democratic (and populist) platforms, their eventual rule was neither democratic nor populist, at least when compared with the governments of Latin America, and could not be accused of pursuing macropopulist policies. The economic growth that took place was often under the aegis of one-party or military rule. Power was concentrated in a tiny, educated elite who quickly divorced themselves from the rest of the population. The authoritarian turn in national politics undermined the political coalitions that had sustained the nationalist movements. It also eroded any accountability the state may have had to the citizenry. Under such conditions, corruption and personalization of public property were rampant. The policy environment was characterized by a lack of consultation with populations.

A considerable volume of literature has attributed the economic failure to these regimes. Unsavoury though the African regimes have been in many ways, this simple attribution of policy failures is not easily borne out by empirical evidence. High and low growth rates have been achieved under very different kinds of government. The SAPs have been pursued by a wide range of regimes. Indeed, in the past, the World Bank expressly showed a preference for the "Banda-types" for their "autonomy" from local publics. One should also recall the inverted-V pattern of Africa's economic performance since independence. One would have to argue that just around the apex of that curve, in the mid-1970s, there was a proliferation of the regime types that accounted for both the crisis and the failure to adjust. It is important to stress this because the challenges facing Africa may defy mere changes in types of regime, as the new African democracies are quickly learning.

Looking back at the last 30 years or so, one is struck by how central politics has been to policy-making. It is, therefore, tempting to blame politics for the African crisis and to somehow seek to get "politics" out of policy-making. However, if there are any lessons to be learned from the disasters in Angola, Liberia, Mozambique, Rwanda, and Somalia, it is that failure to "invest" in politics can be extremely costly. In many African countries, the investment in politics has paid off more than is often realized. The majority of African countries are artificial creations of colonial masters, but they have managed to exist as relatively cohesive nations. Holding together many of the groups that make up many African countries is tough and has often involved a complex balancing act. Poverty is endemic, and distributional consequences of policy actions are critical to provoking or abating crisis. This has implications for economic policy that need to be emphasized. Economic policy that is insensitive to the distributional implications and eschews politics or, even worse, that undermines this delicate cohesion is doomed to fail.

Conclusions

By the mid-1970s, many countries could point to significant progress in initiating processes of economic and social development. Some level of industrialization had been initiated, levels of school enrolment had increased, new roads had been constructed, the indigenization of the civil service had advanced, and so forth. However, it was also clear that the economies were still woefully underdeveloped and vulnerable to global economic change, without the wherewithal for rapid adjustment.

Chapter 2

THE CRISIS
Diagnosis and Prescriptions

The crisis that has engulfed Africa over the last two decades can be traced to the oil crises of 1973 and 1979, which precipitated the recession in the developed countries, declining demand for raw materials, high interest rates, and so forth. The first signs of the impending crisis were the increasing current-account deficits as most African governments chose to finance continued expenditure through borrowing rather than adjusting. The other side of the coin was a much higher level of investment than could be covered by domestic saving. During this period, there was indeed a rupture in the close relationship between savings and investments that had existed in most African countries. It is also important to note that other than Côte d'Ivoire and Zaire, which were eager borrowers in the European currency market, many African countries were ambivalent borrowers that were coached and encouraged by the international financial institutions to borrow in international financial markets (Wellons 1977). By the early 1980s, it became increasingly obvious that these levels of investments and the resource gaps they generated, together with their mirror image in the balance of payments, were unsustainable. African and Latin American countries were abruptly frozen out of international financial markets. Unable to finance their investment programs and unwilling or unable to institute adjustment measures to cope with the abruptly changed circumstances, most countries found themselves in the grip of stagflation.

The most important macroeconomic indicator was the decline in per capita income (see Table 2). At the sectoral level, agriculture continued its decline unabatedly. Part of the decline may have been accounted for by the intensification of the exploitative practices of the states as they sought to maintain absolute amounts of revenue from agriculture during periods of declining world prices. However, the most enduring cause of the decline was the collapse of support to agriculture, especially for rural infrastructure. The decline in public investment in infrastructure further reduced the responsiveness of agriculture to price incentives. Matters were made worse by the droughts that affected most of the countries of the Sahel.

Africa's industrialization initiatives were brought to an abrupt standstill. The growth of manufacturing value added (MVA) over the 1980–93 period was only 3% per annum in real terms, and the rate declined steadily over time, from 3.7% in the first half of the 1980s to 2% between 1989 and 1994. Several studies have suggested that this trend persists. The growth performance conceals the continued stagnation or actual falls in MVA in many countries, particularly those of SSA, as some countries suffered from sustained deindustrialization during the past decade and a half. Africa, the least-industrialized region, suffered the most serious loss in manufacturing capacity in the developing world.

Explaining the crisis

Explanations of the origins of the African crisis have profoundly affected both the nature of the prescriptions and the mutual perceptions of African and donor governments. It is necessary to briefly deal with this wave of "political economy of policy-making" because it affects how one perceives the role of the state in dealing with the crisis. It has also produced a cognitive model of African policy and policy-making that has vitiated initiatives for policy dialogue.

Explaining the African crisis has become a veritable industry and has tended to be polarized between externalist and internalist perspectives, with the former attributing the crisis largely to external factors and the latter pointing to internal policy failures. This is not an academic question. One's understanding of the source of the crisis conditions one's perception of the solution. For instance, those who discount external factors have tended to fail to integrate the secular declines in terms of trade or the instabilities in the global financial and commodity markets into their policy proposals, whereas those who adopt an externalist view underestimate the importance of policy failures.

Policy failures

Differences in performance among developing countries in response to putatively identical crises have revived interest in political economy, which for years was almost exclusively a neo-Marxist preoccupation. Policy failure has become the main focus of analyses conducted by international organizations. Such failure includes

- Indiscriminate allocation of resources and rent-generating resources without any guarantees of reciprocal action by recipients;
- Irresponsible monetary and fiscal policy;
- Failure to maintain physical infrastructure;
- Negligence of markets as an effective means of resource allocation;
- Failure to promote agriculture; and
- Failure to introduce policies to support diversification of exports.

Policy failure has played an important role in the emergence and depth of the African crisis. African governments have over the years increasingly accepted their responsibility for some of these policy failures and have embarked on or accepted reforms to correct them. Much of the current debate on policy demonstrates a reductionist quest for the "ultimate explanation" for policy-making in Africa.

Asserting with Spartan certainty that good policies were known, political economists then asked

- Why do governments find it difficult to embrace programs of economic reform and why do they leave it so late before introducing reform measures?
- Can economic adjustment occur without a simultaneous program of political and administrative reforms?
- What opportunities for coalition politics exist in the promotion of "necessary" economic reforms?
- Which sections of the state elite can be expected to be reliable allies in the quest for market-led reforms?
- How might technocrats be insulated from undesirable interest-group pressures that might compromise the integrity of the adjustment package?

- What capacities exist locally for initiating or grasping orthodox market reforms?
- What lessons can be learned about timing, phasing, and sequencing the implementation of reform policies?

The dominant political-economic response to these questions leans on the idea of the "capture" of policy by societal elements in a manner that particularizes policy and drives it away from the larger societal concerns. This possibility of capture is so dreaded that it informs virtually every claim that the state must be given a minimal role in policy-making. Societal pressures, and more specifically state–society relations, have assumed a great salience in explaining policy failure. It is, therefore, necessary to briefly say something about this issue. If social agency is crucial to development, then one's view of what drives social actors, their organizational capacity, and their relationship to key instruments of policy-making is crucial.

Championed largely by Africanists based in North American universities and immediately embraced by the World Bank as it developed its political-economic analysis of African policy-making, this view takes as its starting point the claim that the postcolonial African state, by its very nature and definition, is at the heart of the economic and governance crises pervading the continent. This state, stripped of the most basic checks and balances of the (late) colonial period, has failed signally in its developmental mission because of various interrelated factors:

- Its "excessive" and "counterproductive" intervention in domestic economic processes, to the detriment of market forces and the private sector;
- Its overbureaucratization and bloated size;
- The domination of its apparatuses by client networks and an "urban coalition" that orients it against the rural (productive) sector and "rational" macroeconomic policies;
- Its submission to "rampant macropopulism" as it panders to the vociferous urban coalition;
- Its monopolization of the main economic levers in society, with the resultant proliferation of rent-generating or rent-seeking niches and activities; and
- Its overcentralization of development, which discourages local (private) initiative.

Underpinning the failure of the postcolonial African state was the capture of the state by societal forces. For some, the exploits of rational individuals pursuing rents or self-interest produced the coalitions behind certain policies. For others, the alliance between local classes and transnational capital pushed the import-substituting process to the absurd stage of stifling exports. For still others, the fault lay essentially with the "neopatrimonial" nature and the rent-generating or rent-seeking motivation of African policymakers. These characteristics have been central to policies that "distort" markets through protectionist tariff and nontariff barriers, misguided industrial development programs, overvalued exchange rates, artificial price-fixing or price controls, a host of subsidies, and preference for state monopolies.

In extending its reach as part of its goal of achieving short-term political order, the state has encouraged the proliferation of patronage institutions and networks that consolidate the position of a legitimacy-hungry elite by enabling it to "buy" the support, acquiescence, or silence of other social forces while it dips its snout deeply and uninterruptedly into the public trough. Given the domination of the economy by the neopatrimonial state or by a neopatrimonialist state logic, it is not surprising that the failure of the state easily translates into the failure of the economy. The fragile patronage structures underpinning the state must constantly be reconstituted, a process that produces acute regime or policy instability and resource misallocation on a stupendous scale, to the detriment of long-term national development.

Policy failure induced partly by some of the factors indicated above did, indeed, play a significant role in creating the African crisis. However, the picture of policy-making in Africa must have more nuances than what emerges in orthodox new political economics if we are to explain some of the paradoxes that have bedeviled this analysis.

First, similar social groups and rent-seeking activities are encountered in countries that have performed well. Indeed, in some of the accounts of the Asian experience, the states' deliberate creation of rents and their transfer to certain groups were central to Asia's high economic performance. Thus, the explanatory power of such activities obviously needs qualification.

Second, in its extreme form, this analysis deduces the existence of interest groups from the mere existence of certain policies from which such groups would benefit. The empirical evidence is usually anecdotal. One effect is that the analysis often runs into paradoxical behavioural patterns, especially when social groups identifed with a particular set of policies by the logic of the model champion an entirely different set.

Third, and more worrisome, is the cynical implication that state officials, politicians, policymakers, and bureaucrats do not have the slightest sense of duty to make them serve anything other than the crass interests of their group or patrons. This is a political analysis so devoid of moral agency that it makes the whole discourse on policy-making meaningless. The current cynicism about an African policy elite excludes from serious consideration several useful things that states ought to be doing in Africa.

Such an approach also leads to denigration and vilification of African civil servants and the justification of policies that have eventually led to their demoralization and noncooperation with foreign-imposed adjustment programs and to a fatal weakening of African bureaucracies. It has led to the much bemoaned loss of policy ownership, now claimed to be essential to policy implementation and sustainability. And worse, it has led to the view that the state is malevolent. The implications of such a view for policy-making are far-reaching. Toye (1994, p. 25) stated the following:

> The state as the source of *all* economic evils was... a convenient
> belief, because it limited the range of bottlenecks and rigidities
> which had to be removed in the course of structural adjustment to
> those which had been created by government policies. From this it
> appeared to follow that, once the correct (neo-liberal policies) are
> followed, all would be well because *all* bottlenecks and rigidities
> would have been removed by the process of liberalisation and
> deregulation. Here lay the source of the widespread, but mistaken,
> optimism about what structural adjustment could achieve. Once
> the idea took general hold that the state was the single source of
> economic failure, a panacea seemed to be possible by simply rolling
> back its boundaries.

The accompanying demonization of local elites suggests, often surreptitiously and at times openly, the need for a *deus ex machina* to devise and implement policies unencumbered with the clamour of domestic politics. From there, it is only a short walk to the conclusion that foreign institutions should take the driver's seat as agents of restraint or that dictators with a "strong political will" should be supported if they produce market-friendly policies.

Fourth, the focus on domestic-policy failures led to a gross underestimation of the role of external factors. This in turn led to a cognitive dissonance among policymakers, who considered the orthodox diagnosis suspect because for them the effects of the external factors were obvious. If foreign experts could not see the most obvious proximate causes of the crisis (such as the dramatic fall in terms of trade for Zambia), then their knowledge was suspect. The combative insistence on internal causes or policy failures contributed to the mistrust that led to the breakdown of the policy dialogue. Later, much later, the international financial institutions conceded, albeit grudgingly and often only after their own programs failed, that external factors had played a role creating the crisis. In the meantime, a deep chasm had been created that made policy dialogue so difficult.

Finally, the approach implies extreme voluntarism. It suggests that policy is merely the result of agency without taking into account structural factors that shape policy and assign to the state certain functions beyond those imposed by a simple arithmetic of interest articulation. By attributing too much to social agency, it pays little attention to the structural and systemic imperatives that state policy must come to grips with in normal circumstances. A state not only must gain legitimacy and ensure the stability of the system by redistributive policies but also must ensure that the reproduction of the economy is sustained by encouraging accumulation and production. This is true even of the most predatory states.

One logical outcome of the analysis was the World Bank's entrance into the arena of political engineering of the most naive kind. A major preoccupation, under the rubric of governance, was to answer two questions:

- Which types of political regime are most suitable for implementing structural adjustment?
- How might the "winners" from structural adjustment be supported to constitute a local resource for the program and how might the "losers" be compensated, outmaneuvred, or sidestepped to prevent them from obstructing the implementation of the program?

The question of how the winners in the reform process could be constituted as a politically feasible and durable coalition for market-based economic policies was soon to flower into a full-scale discussion about the necessity for local ownership of the adjustment programs and how this might be bolstered. This approach to policy failure has generated a whole set of paradoxes.

First, economic reform is a state activity, and such a far-reaching reform requires a strong and capable state. However, if the state is mired in clientalistic relations and if policy goes against the interests of the dominant rent-seeking coalitions to which the state is supposedly beholden, then policy reform will simply not take place. One solution would be to circumvent the state entirely or place faith in a *deus ex machina* of "change teams." Yet, evidence suggests that policy is only implemented if the implementers are active, hence the calls for letting the Africans own the adjustment. To confound matters further, African states are in fact adopting and implementing adjustment, contrary to the predictions of the political economics in vogue.

Second, it is argued that implementation requires "autonomous" states that can implement policies unencumbered by societal pressures, but it is also argued (much less by the BWIs than by the bilaterals) that democracy is essential to good governance.

It should be obvious even from this brief outline that the dominant understanding of the factors that have shaped policies in Africa is too narrow and, ultimately, prevents people from thinking positively about what role the state should play in the adjustment process. Policies have been driven by a host of forces: self-interest, lack of analytical capacity, initial conditions, resource bases, class and other social struggles, simple misreading of a very complex situation, misguided advice of experts, ideological inflexibility, and so forth. There is, therefore, a need for a less reductionist interpretation of policy-making in Africa, one that takes into account agency, structure, and contingency. We briefly turn to this and outline some of the key factors that shape policy-making in Africa.

The logic of nation-building and development imperatives

Given the egregious mismanagement of African economies and the voluminous narratives of such mismanagement, it is difficult to imagine that African policymakers could have been driven by anything other than self-aggrandizement. However, such a view would be doing injustice to many leaders and policymakers who have been deeply committed to the demands of nation-building and development. The exigencies of nation-building, legitimation, and development imposed their own claims on state attention and resources.

Nationalism coloured economic policies in particular ways. First, the nation-state was policy's unit of analysis. As such, the state's preoccupation was with the perceived welfare of its citizens, not with maximizing some global welfare function. Second, the state would tend to favour nationals or would try to remedy inherited imbalances in the ownership of property or access to economic resources. Third, in lieu of an indigenous capitalist class, the state would assume many entrepreneurial tasks regardless of its overall ideological position.

Much has been written on the relationship between nationalism, the exigencies of nation-building, and policy (Myrdal 1957; Bronfenbrenner, 1958; Johnson 1967; Ake 1979; Schatzenberg 1980). Suffice it to note that nationalist impulses partially explain the policies that have been identified exclusively with rent-seeking (nationalization, import substitution, expenditure on education, panterritorial pricing, and so forth). Thus, nationalism could simultaneously account for some of the sacrifices and commitment behind successes and some of the chauvinism and xenophobia behind disasters. Significantly, nationalism influences the perceptions that policies are externally imposed or likely to compromise national sovereignty or unity.

Policy-making in Africa has been affected by the dominant interpretation of causes of underdevelopment. For much of the 1960s and 1970s, African policymakers and the aid donors that provided the key technical assistance were generally persuaded of the validity of the "structuralist" elements of policies behind, for example, import substitutions. Armed with that perspective, African governments with any developmental pretensions adopted a series of policies to address the perceived structural constraints on development. Expenditures on social and physical infrastructure went up; protective measures for infant industries were introduced; tax incentives to attractive foreign capital were initiated; and in response to the reticence of private investors, state industries were put in place to jump-start the industrialization process.

Development in this sense also demanded a strong and active state. At the time when most African countries attained independence, the international environment was decidedly in favour of state interventionism in the development process. This was essentially as true for the centrally planned economies of the East bloc as it was for their capitalist rivals in the West. It was also as true for the developing countries as it was for the developed countries. As it pertained to the developing countries, including those of Africa, a variety of theories, ranging from the "big-push" approach to the Gershenkron thesis, were developed and popularized in support of an interventionist role for the state in the struggle against underdevelopment.

The strength of such an approach was that it addressed real markets, with their rigidities, failures, incompleteness, and so forth. And for all the peremptory dismissal of it by the neoliberals, it constituted a fairly accurate stylization of underdevelopment. Recent concern with growth and development has begun to revive interest in this perspective's principal preoccupations — accumulation, externalities, structural rigidities, etc. In an interventionist framework, however, this approach suffered several limitations that vitiated the thrust of policies based on it.

The first limitation was that it paid too little attention to short-term macroeconomic variables and, consequently, gave low priority to fiscal and monetary issues and the management of balance-of-payments problems.

A second limitation was related to the failure to design mid-term strategies to serve as a bridge between the short-term fiscal, monetary, and trade policies and the long-term development strategy. More specifically, it had no instruments to deal with short-term shocks that moved the economy away from the targeted path. Development economics, with its linear view of movement from one stage to another, never incorporated "business cycles" and macroeconomic manifestations in its analysis. And although it recognized that external shocks were usually a source of instability, no set of tools was developed to deal with such an eventuality. The result was that once the economy was off its course, a flurry of ad hoc measures and stop–go policies were adopted, often leading to even greater destabilization of the economy.

A third limitation was the failure to articulate state–market relations in a way that would best use the strengths of each of these institutions. Part of this neglect of the market came from the prevalence of market failure, the nonexistence of certain key markets, and the foreign domination of functioning markets. For all these reasons, market forces were underrated as an instrument of industrialization. Further, with respect to long-term accumulation, it did seem that market-based decisions were too myopic to allow for the kind of far-sighted decisions that development required.

A final limitation was its naive assumption about states and social interests. Its social-engineering mode failed to take into account the politics of setting the social-welfare function, of creating a society in which everyone is equal before the law, or of building state capacity, not only in terms of technical competency but also in terms of eliciting support from the citizenry on the basis of the state's legitimacy.

Interest groups and classes

Interest groups and social classes have played a central role in policy-making in Africa. However, because of the relative novelty of these groups and the multiplicity of their identities and interests, attempts to monotonically link policies to particular interest groups or social classes or fractions of such classes tend to be too simplistic and often tautological. Much of the association of policy with particular groups is arrived at deductively and usually without evidence that policy changes were demanded by a coherent interest group or class. The usual procedure is to simply assume that if a group benefited from a particular policy, the group must have pushed for it. In many cases, however, the social groups identified with certain policies have actually been spawned by the policies they are supposed to have pushed for. An associated hypothesis is that all interests can ultimately be reduced to economic interests. Under this assumption, people cease to exist as moral agents with passions and social identities that transcend the aggregates of the arithmetic of individual pursuit of material good. In a continent where politics must manage not only the pressures of different interest groups but also the passions engendered by other social realities such as ethnicity and gender, such reductionist materialism impoverishes the understanding of the complexities of policy-making in Africa. One should add here, however, that local classes and interest groups usually have had to contend with international actors to gain the attention of policymakers. This was, of course, the point of much of the "dependency school," although the manner in which these contests manifest themselves today is much more apparent because of the greater involvement of international financial institutions in policy-making.

Resource base and policy option

In the stylized discussion on policy choice and performance, it is usually asserted that whereas the successful countries chose export-oriented industrialization, African countries chose inward-looking import substitution. Studies are then conducted to establish how export performance was good for growth and how import substitution led to stagnation. The reasons behind the choices are equally occluded by the suggestion that in one case it was the autonomy of the state that allowed it to pursue an export-oriented strategy, whereas ISI is evidence of rent-seeking and patronal–clientalist relationships.

Reading the histories of the Asian and African countries, however, one is struck by a number of similarities. In both cases, industrialization stood high on the list of priorities. Both groups assumed the state would play a central role in encouraging import substitution. Both sought to transform their export structures from ones based on traditional exports to ones based on more diversified, industry-based exports. The great difference was in how each group perceived the means to financing industrialization — more specifically, how to acquire the foreign-exchange earnings needed to purchase machinery and technology.

In the simple two-factors-of-production world (capital and labour or capital and land), the advice is quite straightforward. To earn the necessary foreign exchange for industrialization, capital-poor, labour-rich countries should "export" the labour embodied in labour-intensive activities. Similarly, the land-abundant economies must "export" land in the form of minerals, agricultural produce, or tourism to provide the foreign exchange for industrialization.

In a three-factor world of labour, land, and capital, the situation becomes a little more complicated. The appropriate combination of land with capital and labour is not as easy to specify because, in some cases, economies of scale and the availability of technologies will play an important role in the choice of techniques. On the basis of simple comparative advantage, therefore, economies will tend to cluster around the three apexes of the resource triangle (Figure 3).

Given the land shortage in most Asian countries, the pressures to create employment were enormous. More significantly, the only way to export labour to acquire the necessary foreign exchange for industrialization was through the export of labour embodied in labour-intensive manufactures. For the many land-abundant African countries, the obvious strategy was to increase the output of mineral and agricultural produce for export. For instance, Nkrumah's government, for which industrialization was the cornerstone of economic policy, doubled Ghana's output of cocoa between 1957 and 1966 to increase foreign-exchange availability. The choice was based on existing capacity and projections of future prices for raw materials that, as it turned out, were wide of the mark. It was only during the mid-1970s that the employment problem entered the policy agenda in Africa because the relatively high growth rates turned out to be accompanied by equally rapid labour absorption.

These self-evident, comparative-advantage-based policy options had different implications for the development potentials of the countries because they had different effects on skill formation, manifestation of externalities, and cost reduction for the economy as a whole. In the various countries, the initial choices virtually locked onto different paths and in many ways determined the subsequent capacities to adjust to crises. A considerable amount of literature relates policy-making and performance to resource bases (see, for instance, Shaffer 1994; Auty 1995; Mkandawire 1995; Lal 1996). This literature suggests how natural resources affect the fiscal base and capacity of the state, the flexibility of the production structure, the use of labour, the organizational base of interest groups, and so forth. Although some of this literature tends to lapse into extremes of geographical determinism (see, for instance, Sachs 1997), it serves as a useful antidote to the rather voluntaristic discourse on state policy in Africa. Lal (1996), using a model that classifies countries as land abundant, labour abundant, or intermediate, noted that during the post-1973 crisis, 8 out of 10 countries in the land-abundant group suffered a collapse — the exceptions were Malaysia and Thailand. On the other hand, none in the labour-abundant group and only three in the intermediate-endowment group (Jamaica, Madagascar, and Peru) suffered a growth collapse.

Figure 3. The resource triangle.

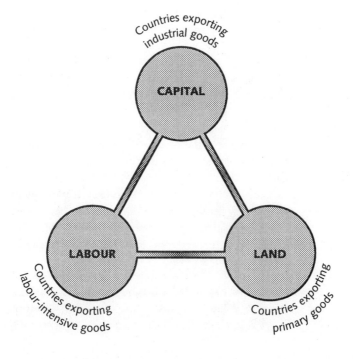

One should also recall here the difficulties of sustaining economic development associated with natural-resource abundance. If, at first sight, the presence of natural resources provides an opportunity to finance economic growth, it also brings problems that can block development:

- The existence of natural resources tends to divert attention from the development of human resources, a crucial ingredient in long-run growth and technical flexibility of the economy. Even in cases where the natural resource is agricultural, the tendency is to increase output more by extensive use of land resources than through the improvement of human capital.

- Natural resources tend to reduce the state to being a *rentier* state relying on an enclave for its revenues. This reliance on rents has two immediate consequences. One is the state attracts fierce battles over the distribution of these rents. The other is there are no obvious reasons to invest productively in other sectors. Investment in other sectors is largely driven by distributive, rather than productive, objectives, especially where the *rentier* nature of the state combines with a strong civil society (Mkandawire 1995).

- To the extent that natural-resource economies can earn the states foreign exchange from export, they tend to be less concerned about making industry earn its own or part of its own foreign exchange. No pressure is exerted to turn import-substituting industries into export-oriented ones. As a result, import substitution is pushed beyond the extent to which it makes economic sense, even given the "infant-industries" argument. This is because such economies are initially able to carry the burden of an uncompetitive manufacturing sector (Auty 1995).

- The enclave nature of the production units and their capital intensity tend to worsen income distribution, which can in turn be a brake on growth.

- Reliance on natural resource-based exports exposes the economy to great instability because prices of raw materials have greater variance and fluctuation than those of manufactured goods. This in turn leads to recurrent import instability, which negatively affects overall economic growth.

- As a result of success in the export of one commodity, the state can become afflicted with the Dutch Disease (the appreciation of domestic currency stifles the export opportunities of other tradable goods).

In the African context, countries such as Gabon, Nigeria, Zaire, and Zambia are familiar with these constraints. The point is not that natural-resource abundance makes development impossible — after all, countries such as Indonesia, Malaysia, and Thailand seem to have deployed their natural resources in a less binding manner than African countries have.

Rather, the point is to underscore one of the many objective factors that focused policy in Africa and the importance of natural resources in shaping policies and the perception of policy options, especially in light of the voluntaristic interpretations of policy-making in Africa.

One should also stress that what most African governments did was simply to base their ISI on their comparative advantage, despite their putative subscription to the Prebisch thesis about the tendency for secular decline in commodity prices. If there is a puzzle, here it is: Why did African policy-makers and their countless advisers not foresee that long-term industrialization prospects could not be tied to the foreign-exchange earnings of so vulnerable a sector? It is important to recall all this because what we are witnessing under the SAPs in a number of key cases is the revival of that focus on natural resources as the expansion of traditional exports is encouraged. (We say this while fully recognizing the discourse on nontraditional exports. In most cases, what this refers to is the addition of a new primary commodity to the traditional exports.) Ghana is back to gold, cocoa, and timber, and Zambia is reviving its copper mining. Most of the new investment in Africa is going back into mining, not so much because of policy changes as because of the global demand for minerals. All this is going on as development of human resources and industrial activities withers. Unless policies are deliberately introduced to relax the focus on natural-resource exports and to conscientiously use mineral wealth to develop human resources and more diversified, labour-absorbing activities, African countries will be embarking on a course of structural inflexibility and vulnerability to terms-of-trade instability. African countries may simply be put back on the track that made them so vulnerable to economic fluctuations and crises.

Technical assistance — too many cooks

One reason for policy failure in Africa is simply that too many cooks have been in the policy-making kitchen. As a former World Bank vice president noted, "the extraordinary fact is that there are more expatriate advisers in Africa today than there were at the end of the colonial period" (Jaycox 1993, p. 9). No part of the developing world has had such a density and diversity of technical assistance as Africa. In some countries, ministries were literally partitioned among different donors. This had many implications. Not only did it tax the attention of the nascent African bureaucracies to the extreme, but it also made the learning curve extremely costly. In the extreme cases, African policymakers were actually excluded from the learning process as donors kept the evaluations of the programs to themselves, either through exclusive distribution of the relevant documents or because of language barriers. In apparent frustration regarding the treatment of United Nations Economic Commission for Africa (UNECA) initiatives, Professor Adedeji, then Executive Secretary of UNECA, lamented,

> In many cases, our friends and development partners have been either unwilling or reluctant to grant us the elementary right to perceive for ourselves what is good for us and to assist us in realising our perceived goals and objectives. Often, they appear more interested in foisting on us their own perceptions and goals. When it comes to Africa, the outsiders have always behaved as if they know better than Africans what is good for Africa, and the result is that without the needed co-operation and support, Africa has particularly always been derailed from pursuing relentlessly and vigorously the agenda it has set for itself, whether it is the Monrovia Strategy, the Lagos Plan of Action or the Final Act of Lagos.

Sachs (1996, p. 20) agreed:

> Since independence, African countries have looked to donor nations — often their former colonial rulers — and to the international financial institutions for guidance on growth. Indeed, since the onset of the African debt crisis of the 1980s, the guidance has become a kind of economic receivership, with the policies of many African nations decided in a seemingly endless cycle of meetings with the IMF [International Monetary Fund], the World Bank, donors and creditors. What a shame. So many good ideas, so few results. ... Africa is constantly berated for its poor politics and bad economic ideas, though much of the mischief has come from the outside. In the 1960s, the fad at the World Bank and among many donors was "development planning." In the 1970s, this gave way to "basic needs," a doctrine which led the World Bank to support the socialist strategies of soon-to-be-bankrupt Tanzania and other non-market economies. In the 1980s, "basic needs" was supplanted by "structural adjustment" which rightly focused on markets but neglected to set priorities in the reform. In the ensuing frustration, the focus in the

1990s has shifted to "good governance": donors now berate African governments for their "lack of ownership" of reforms dictated by the IMF and World Bank.

It is estimated that about 100 000 expatriate technical-assistance staff work in Africa, meddling in every aspect of policy analysis, advice, policy-making, and implementation and gulping up $4 billion USD per annum (Stewart 1995). According to Helleiner (1994, p. 10),

> Foreign donors both "drive" and "own" technical cooperation in Africa. It is a costly, inefficient and increasingly "unsettling" device for overcoming domestic budget constraints and government employment freezes. This degree of intrusion into domestic policy formation and the concomitant failure to develop appropriate local research and decision-making capacity is not found, and would not be tolerated, elsewhere in the developing world.

It is remarkable to observe how Africa, over the decades, has been the pawn of international interests experimenting with development models. Most countries have followed passively; at each turn, previous policies implemented with all the technical assistance and massive support of the donor agencies have been berated as Africa's mistakes, and new policies are recommended. Africa's problem has not been its failure to learn but its learning too well from all and sundry.

The SAPs have in many ways compounded the problems by multiplying the number of experts. Moreover, these cooks were not master chefs. Some were already disastrous performers as aid givers in various projects, and the move to macroeconomic policy was both an expression of project fatigue and an excuse for the failure of projects. Also, whereas the International Monetary Fund (IMF) could boast of experience in stabilizing individual economies, the World Bank assumed the chef's role with no demonstrated experience in structurally adjusting an economy to induce accelerated development. These institutions were "badly prepared protagonists of modest ability employing data of dubious quality and entering upon a series of battles over very complex policy questions" (Helleiner 1994). The African side was probably no better, but as Hutchful (1995) observed, "in this discourse of the blind the side with the money usually won."

One can grasp from all this that the determinants of policy in Africa have been more complex than the more cynical accounts of African policy-making suggest. Also, the naive social engineering in search of change teams or autonomous bureaucrats not only is misleading and doomed to fail but also is founded on an ahistorical and ideologically driven understanding of states in Africa.

One should also note that the nature of failure is not as evident as might be suggested. For those of neoclassical persuasion, policy failure is virtually inherent to state policy. Protection of industry, "financial repression," and state ownership of industry all constitute distortionary elements and are evidence of wrong policies ineluctably bound to fail. Yet, each of these elements was a constituent part of the policies of the high-performing Asian economies. Even in Africa, some of the good performance of the past can be attributed to these policies. One should also watch against the conflation of macro- and microeconomic policies. As Rodrik (1995) argued, the propensity to fall into crisis is not correlated with the nature of microeconomic policies proper. Many of the microeconomic policies that are condemned were successfully used in the Asian economies. If African economies have failed, it was largely due to the lack of selectivity and flexibility in the use of these instruments and the absence of a coherent strategy for applying them. In the debate over policy, virtually every policy initiative — macro or micro — that was taken during the dirigiste era is condemned. The "guilty by association" condemnation of many central elements of industrial policy has led to the neglect of existing industry and to unnecessary waste. Even more ominous for Africa's future industrialization prospects is that the SAPs have left African governments with virtually nothing to do for industry except prepare it for privatization or closure.

Other external factors

We noted earlier how the external environment of the 1960–75 period favoured an accumulation process that was based on import substitution mainly financed by earnings from exports of primary products. Impressive though the rates of growth of many African countries were, the economies remained highly vulnerable. Elbadawi and Ndulu (1996) emphasized the extreme vulnerability of growth in Africa, as well as of African domestic policy, to the magnitude and variability of external shocks. Shocks to African economies are largely related to structural dependence on imports to sustain production and investment, on uncertain revenue from exports, and on exogenous revenues to finance them. Ironically, with import substitution, imports increasingly consist of essential intermediary and capital goods. Consequently, this compression of imports leads to a decline in production because there is little room for reduction of discretionary-consumption goods.

The other external factors analyzed by Elbadawi and Ndulu (1996) were terms of trade, changes in interest rates, and net transfer effects (that is, net capital inflow of debt payment and other transfers abroad). The Elbadawi–Ndulu study found that from 1970 to 1990, terms of trade clearly dominated, accounting for an income loss of 3.8% of GDP, twice the 1.9% loss for other developing countries. The study further reported that 1973–76 and 1987–89 witnessed the most severe terms-of-trade shocks. Because the price changes were larger and because the share of imports in GDP was higher, import price increases were more significant causes of terms-of-trade shocks during 1973–75 and in 1979 and 1980. Between 1970 and 1990, Africa suffered a net income loss of 2.1% from all these shocks combined. For the other developing countries, the loss was 1.6%.

A most disturbing realization is that the much disparaged Prebisch–Singer thesis on the secular decline holds and that what Africa has been experiencing may be this secular trend. (Several studies cited in Elbadawi and Ndulu [1996] used sophisticated econometric methods to confirm the Prebisch–Singer thesis.) Although the import-substituting strategies were often partly based on this thesis, African governments never fully drew out the central implication, namely, that they should speed up their diversification into nontraditional exports. Current adjustment policies, based on denigrating the export pessimism of the Prebisch–Singer thesis and on a desire to get the African economies earning foreign exchange, are reviving Africa's comparative advantage and steering it into the same traditional activities without taking into account this feature of commodity-price behaviour.

Insistence on the importance of external factors has generally been treated as merely scapegoating. To be sure, policymakers have too often shirked their responsibilities by conveniently blaming outsiders. Our intention here is not to rationalize, let alone ignore the infamous mismanagement of economies by African governments. Rather, the point is to emphasize that successful adjustment will be elusive unless Africa's vulnerability to external factors is recognized. Such a recognition will serve in rethinking the form and content of Africa's structural transformation. Failure to account for such factors, even as one corrects internal policy errors, can frustrate attempts at change and condemn them to involuntary reversal.

Most observers would today agree that both internal policy errors and external factors played a role in causing or aggravating the African crisis. They would also agree that the initial conditions under which African economies embarked on adjustment strategies in response to the crisis made adjustment a particularly difficult task. Although concessions have been made on all sides, the source of the African crisis is still contested, and this polarization still shows up. Differences in emphasis (sometimes even by the same institutions and individuals) are frequent and yield extremely polarized prescriptions. For a whole range of reasons, the view that dominates policy-making is the one that attributes the lion's share of the blame for the crisis and its persistence to policy failure. In *Adjustment in Africa*, the World Bank (1994, p. 20) was quite categorical about this:

> The main factors behind the stagnation and decline were poor policies — both macroeconomic and sectoral and emanating from a development paradigm that gave the state a prominent role in production and in regulating economic activity.

External factors are recognized, but they are downplayed as simply "surmountable obstacles." Thus, SAPs, despite their perfunctory acknowledgment of external factors, are based on essentially internalist arguments that, in turn, are based firmly on a neoclassical vision of the economy.

In sum, policy-making in Africa has been driven by a wide range of forces. Concentration on rent-seeking or clientalism, although pointing to real problems of institutional failure in Africa, not only is too simplistic but also produces a state of mind that denigrates the actions of virtually all social actors and ultimately leads to paralysis of action.

Prescriptions

Given the external shocks that fundamentally altered the configurations of international economic relations and thus made existing policies of most less-developed countries obsolete, and given the past policy mistakes that accentuated the crisis and the weaknesses of domestic institutions to deal with the new challenges, it became evident that SSA countries needed one form of adjustment or another. What was not evident was what form would work. Indeed, the major source of interminable debate was the insistence by the BWIs that a certain kind of reform was the only feasible alternative and better than any other conceivable option.

The ascendence of neoliberalism on a global scale spilled over into the African situation largely through the BWIs. Two major historical events combined to make the SAPs the dominant model of economic management in most developing countries in the early 1980s.

First, there was the apparent loss of faith in neo-Keynesian economics in the late 1970s and the intellectual ascendancy of the new classical economics and the principle of "monoeconomics" as the dominant paradigm for diagnosing economic problems and prescribing solutions. Such neoclassical interpretation is based on the theoretical and empirical corpus of work that essentially derives from a set of theories explaining the efficacy of the market system in resource allocation. Its major principle is that of monoeconomics, which insists on the universality of rational economic behaviour and the existence of marginal substitution possibilities in production and consumption.

Second, in the major industrialized countries, there was a strong political attack on big government as being both incompetent and oppressive, and this was reinforced by the evident failure of centralized planning in the former Soviet Union and other communist countries in the 1980s. This attack dovetailed neatly with the twin concepts of efficiency and market forces, and the neoclassical paradigm provided the anchor. Consequently, more conservative leaders were elected in major industrial countries — Margaret Thatcher in Britain (1979), Joe Clark in Canada (1980), Ronald Reagan in the United States (1980), and Helmut Kohl in Germany (1981).

These two events provided the immediate impetus for the obdurate pursuit of the neoclassical agenda as the universally applicable model of development. The broad principles of the neoclassical orthodoxy and its insistence on the "microfoundations to macroeconomics" are taken to be so self-evident that the details are seldom spelled out explicitly. The markets are believed to be efficient, whereas government intervention in resource allocation is distortionary and inefficient. Government failure is more costly and dominates market failure. Minimal government intervention, especially in the provision of infrastructure and education, can be undertaken provided such intervention is functional, or "market friendly." Under this framework, "rolling back the state" and "unleashing the markets" are the key phrases on the reform agenda.

In the case of Africa, the Berg report (World Bank 1981) provided the immediate intellectual precursor to the introduction of SAP policies. According to the report, the observed declines in Africa's standard of living were not due to vagaries of weather, political conflict, and external shocks but arose from mistakes in economic policy-making. Hence, the Berg report identified "three major policy actions that are central to any growth-oriented program: (a) more suitable trade and exchange-rate policies; (b) increased efficiency of resource use in the public sector; and (c) improvement in agricultural policies" (World Bank 1981, p. 3).

Consequently, as is typical of such reform programs in developing countries, two broad policy components come to characterize the typical SAP package: short- to medium-term macroeconomic stabilization measures to restore internal and external balances, which falls within the province of the IMF; and SAPs proper, which are designed to "unleash markets so that competition can help improve the allocation of resources... getting price signals right and creating a climate that allows businesses to respond to those signals in ways that increase the returns to investment" (World Bank 1994, p. 61).

Unleashing markets

Since the early 1980s, several African countries have pursued SAPs with varying degrees of intensity, commitment, and longevity. There is now much greater reliance on markets. The central message of the SAPs has been "get the prices right, unleash the markets, and rein in the state." Here, we briefly outline some principal components of the SAPs.

INDUSTRIAL-POLICY REFORMS

Industrial policy is a summary term encompassing activities of government intended to develop or retrench various industries in a national economy to maintain global competitiveness. If there is any sector in which the World Bank has exhibited ambiguity, it is the industrial sector. "Industrial policy" in Africa is generally viewed as the linchpin of the import-substituting strategy that the SAPs sought to dismantle. In the Berg report (World Bank 1981), industry received very little attention beyond being listed as evidence of the waste and inefficiency of past policies. In another report, the World Bank (1989b) recognized that industrialization in Africa has achieved little indigenous technological development and proposed greater emphasis on acquiring the necessary entrepreneurial, managerial, and technical skills. Incentives should focus on training and technological adaptations. Proposing a new start to industrialization, the report correctly identified the challenge as one of building on the base of technical skills and industrial experience already in place to achieve the industrial transformation envisioned in the Lagos Plan of Action. African entrepreneurship would be fostered through improvements in the business regulatory and policy environment, expansion of access to credit, encouragement of self-sustaining services (for example, technical services and subcontracting), and stimulation of local markets. Charting a strategic agenda for the 1990s, the report recommended that adjustment programs account more fully for investment needs to accelerate growth and stated that the goal of macroeconomic balance must be to fundamentally transform Africa's production structures.

In a fundamental sense, however, the World Bank was averse to industrial policy and denied its usefulness even in the high-performing Asian economies (World Bank 1993). In line with this deep-rooted anti-industrial-policy position, the promising progress exhibited in the 1989 report toward understanding the poor industrial performance in Africa was countered by the 1994 World Bank report. This was a retrogression and reaffirmed that, despite the rhetoric, the core of industrial policy has been, as contained in the Berg report (World Bank 1981), an end to ISI and a greater reliance on the market for identification of promising industries.

AGRICULTURAL REFORMS

Agriculture is the single most important sector of the economy in most African countries both because of its share in GDP and, more significantly, because the population derives much of its livelihood from agriculture. As we noted earlier, this is also the sector that for much of the postcolonial period has experienced continuous decline. Obviously, this sector provides the litmus test for any adjustment policies. SAPs have often been based on inducing African economies to exploit their "revealed" comparative advantage, which has largely been identified with agriculture. The diagnosis of the poor performance has attributed much of the failure to the price policies pursued by African governments, which have taxed agricultural producers.

The Berg report (World Bank 1981) made turning around the decline in agriculture the centrepiece of its arguments. It argued that agricultural output is the single most important determinant of overall economic growth in Africa. The World Bank's recommendations revolved around "getting the prices right." The report recommended improving the terms of trade by abolishing the various export taxes, removing protection of nonagricultural activities, and devolving foreign exchange. Many countries have moved in that direction in the last few years. Reform here has largely involved market liberalization. The state's monopsonistic position, usually manifested as marketing boards, has been drastically reduced. Food subsidies and artificial price ceilings have been removed. Credit ceilings in favour of agriculture have been removed, and so have subsidies for inputs.

FINANCIAL REFORMS

In few areas has the axiomatic mode of thinking about policy led to as much misguidance as it has in the area of finance. This is apparently because, in this sector, one finds a logical construct in which stabilization, through its effects on interest rates, leads to growth by acting on saving, investments, and allocation of resources. The role of interest rates in determining investment, and hence economic growth, has been a matter of controversy for a long time. What constitutes an appropriate interest-rate policy is still a puzzling issue. Until the early 1970s, the main line of argument was that because interest rates represent the cost of capital, low interest rates encourage people to acquire physical capital (investment) and thus promote economic growth. Therefore, during this era, the policy of low real interest rates was adopted by many countries, including the developing countries of Africa. This position was, however, challenged by what is now known as the financial-repression theory, an orthodox approach to financial liberalization that suggests that high positive real interest rates will encourage people to save. This will lead in turn to more investment and economic growth; the classical assumption is that savings are required before investments can be made.

This orthodox approach brought into focus not only the relationship between investment and real interest rates but also that between the real interest rate and saving. It is argued that financial repression, which is often associated with negative real deposit rates, leads to the withdrawal of funds from the banking sector. The reduction in credit availability, it is argued, reduces actual investment and hinders growth. Because of this complementarity between saving and investment, the basic teaching of the orthodox approach is to free deposit rates. Positive real interest rates will encourage saving, and the increased liabilities of the banking system will oblige financial institutions to lend more resources for productive investment in a more efficient way. Higher loan rates, which follow higher deposit rates, will also discourage investment in low-yielding projects and raise the productivity of investment. This orthodox view became highly influential in the design of IMF–World Bank financial liberalization programs that many African countries implemented under the umbrella of the SAPs.

Financial-sector reforms have also included the following (Inanga and Ekpenyong 1998; Mwega 1998):

- Reducing direct and indirect taxation of financial institutions through reserve requirements, mandatory credit ceilings, and credit-allocation guidelines;
- Reducing barriers to competition in the financial sector by scaling down government ownership (through privatization) and by facilitating entry into the sector by domestic and foreign firms; and
- Restructuring or liquidating insolvent banks.

TRADE REFORMS

The opening up of putatively closed African economies has been one of the major tasks of the SAPs. One of the objectives of the SAPs was to improve the rate of export and the performance of the foreign-trade sector by making it competitive through exchange-rate reforms and exposure to global competition. Governments have lowered tariffs, devalued currencies, liberalized trade, and made their economies more open.

LABOUR-MARKET REFORMS

It has been part of orthodoxy to argue that African labour markets have been rendered inflexible largely by minimum wages, job security, social-security contributions, unemployment benefits, trade unions, and so forth. The International Labor Organization (ILO 1996, p. 193) summarized this view:

> The orthodox view maintains that such interventions raise the cost of labour in the formal sector and hence reduce demand, exacerbate inequalities between formal and informal sectors and impede adjustment to economic shocks by reducing employment and wage flexibility, reduce international competitiveness by raising the cost of labour, and reduce the rate of growth by lowering returns to investment. Removing labour market distortions, it is argued, would enhance labour market flexibility "and have a positive effect on economic growth in developing countries."

The SAPs have consequently included measures to remove all these institutional arrangements from the labour market.

Social-sector reforms

EDUCATION

The World Bank plays a major role in defining education policies in Africa, not only by providing direct funding and tying up local counterpart funds in the direction of its choice but also by providing the intellectual basis for the new policy directions in African economies. With the weakening of such institutions as the United Nations Educational, Scientific and Cultural Organization, the World Bank pronouncements on education have become decisive. World Bank policies on education have been largely influenced by the literature on the rate of return on education (RORE), which provides a market-compatible rationale of state expenditures on education. A vast research program on measuring ROREs has emerged. The World Bank has been an important participant in this research and has drawn some conclusions from it that Bennell (1996) summarized:

- ROREs for all levels of education generally exceed the aggregate social opportunity cost of capital;
- ROREs in developing countries (and especially Africa) are higher than in the advanced market economies;
- The private and social ROREs are highest for primary education;
- Private ROREs for higher education are usually considerably higher than the corresponding social ROREs; and
- The pattern of ROREs remains stable as countries develop, with only relatively minor declines in ROREs.

For Africa, World Bank studies have concluded that the social ROREs are 24% for primary education, 18% for secondary, and 11% for tertiary. From these values and the allegedly universal patterns, the World Bank has drawn policy implications that in turn will have far-reaching implications for Africa's long-term human-resource development. Bennell (1996, p. 183) summed up these policy implications:

> First, all education at whatever level is a relatively attractive investment not only for individuals but for government. Second, with certain caveats, "in most developing countries primary education should receive the highest investment priority, followed by secondary education." Third, government subsidisation of higher, and to a lesser extent secondary education is excessive given the large differentials that exist between private and social ROREs. To remedy this misallocation of resources students should be made to contribute significantly more to the costs of their education.

In addition to the arguments on RORES, the World Bank maintains an equity consideration that militates against public expenditure on higher education and favours private provision of higher education that is "equitable," because government subsidies for higher education are disproportionately high for families that have comfortable incomes and could afford to pay a greater share of university fees (Bennell 1996).

ADMINISTRATIVE REFORMS

In specifying the elements that were thought to be essential for the attainment of "good" governance in Africa, World Bank staff identified the following key principles and parameters:

- Greater accountability (financial and political) of public officials, including politicians and civil servants;
- Transparency in governmental procedures and processes;
- A concerted attack on corruption;
- Predictability in governmental behaviour and in the political system;
- Rationality in governmental decisions;
- Competent auditing of governmental transactions;
- Drastic curbing of bureaucratic red tape;
- Elimination of "unnecessary" administrative controls, to plug avenues for rent-seeking;
- Free flow of information;
- Encouragement of a culture of public debate;
- Institution of a system of checks and balances within the governmental structure;
- Decentralization of government;
- Respect for human rights;
- Judicial autonomy and the rule of law;
- Establishment of a reliable legal framework;
- Protection of property; and
- Enforcement of contracts.

Bank officials also added the issue of capacity-building to enable African technocrats to initiate and implement market-based economic reforms as an essential element of the quest for good governance in Africa. As of the end of 1994, the World Bank was supporting various civil-service reforms in 29 African countries.

In addition to measures such as promoting open, competitive tendering for the supply of goods and services to the government by the private sector, including nongovernmental organizations (NGOs), the World Bank sought to improve transparency in the governmental process by encouraging several African countries to publish official gazettes advertising public tenders and announcing their award. Governments were also encouraged, as in Kenya, to publish a summary version of their annual budget plans for circulation locally. This practice was expected to stimulate public debate on the economy and the public-expenditure pattern adopted by the incumbent regime. In a bid to encourage "informed" reporting and public discussion of economic-reform issues, the World Bank's Economic Development Institute developed training programs for journalists invited from time to time from various African countries. Publications from the World Bank were also routinely disseminated to the media in all of the adjusting countries of Africa, and briefing sessions were regularly scheduled to explain the objectives of the economic-reform process, the recorded successes, and the persistent problems.

The World Bank's work in the area of institution-building was extended, in principle and in practice, to support for grass-roots organizations. These organizations are seen as feasible replacements for the state in several spheres; they are also central to the Bank's strategy for empowering the people and "thickening" civil society as a counterweight to the (neo) patrimonial state. Not only was the establishment of NGOs and grass-roots organizations explicitly encouraged in various African countries but attempts were also made to make them beneficiaries of procurement contracts awarded by the state and of project funds supplied by donors, including the World Bank.

It is important to remember the perceptions behind these reforms. The civil servants were seen as inherently opposed to reform, and in many ways local bureaucracies, who were seen as enemies of the market, were immediately beset with hostility. Vilified as corrupt, rent seeking, and inefficient, local civil servants were to be kept out of the restructuring exercise. In the light of these attitudes, local bureaucracies were skeptical about later suggestions that they "won" the adjustment process.

Chapter 3

The Adjustment Experience

Results

The reason for implementing policy reform is, of course, to influence the targeted economic variable; the corresponding change in this target variable would then serve as an indicator of policy effect. In principle, therefore, the effect of any policy reform can be assessed by examining the changes in appropriate target variables that can be ascribed to policy reform. For several reasons, the impact-evaluation procedure is not as straightforward as it may, at first, appear (see Hussain 1994).

First, it may be virtually impossible to disentangle the effects of policy reform from those emanating from more general exogenous developments that may affect the same set of variables. Exogenous shocks that are unexpected or were not built into adjustment programs can have a significant effect on their success. If world prices of key commodity exports decline appreciably, or rainfall is lower than expected, it would be unfair to attribute poor economic and social performance to the adjustment program alone. The World Bank has been constrained to appeal to these external factors to explain why its own policies have not performed as well as expected. Response to adjustment has been constrained by other such external factors as losses from declining terms of trade, deepening debt, recession in the member countries of the Organisation for Economic Co-operation and Development and, more recently, by the tumultuous process of political transition that has diverted the attention of policy-makers from economic management, leading in some instances to a virtual breakdown of normal economic activity. In several adjusting countries, the external funding promised by donors or the debt relief projected under the program has not materialized. This shortcoming has had a negative effect on imports and, consequently, on the growth of output and exports and the level of public spending. One should take this factor fully into account when judging the success of the adjustment program or its social consequences.

Second, reform episodes in particular countries may be too short to permit an evaluation based essentially on an analysis of time-series data. Critics of the SAPs often argue that the time horizon of these programs has been too short to address deep-seated structural problems. The World Bank now admits that the original premise that these programs would enable economies to revive growth and consumption in 5–7 years was overopti-mistic. The intensity of the distortions and of the demands made on the response capacity of African economies was underestimated.

Third, whether a discernible policy-reform episode can be found may depend significantly on whether private agents (whose actions or in-action ultimately determine "supply response" to policy change) regard the policy as credible and, hence, sustainable.

Fourth, attributing postreform changes in the target variables to the preceding reform effort based on the well-known before-and-after com-parisons is unrelated to appropriate counterfactuals and can be criticized on this account. There is always a problem of how much observed perfor-mance can be ascribed to particular policies where so many things are all happening at once, where exogenous forces are strong, where time lags are important, and where data sources are not completely reliable. This is even more problematic in the food and agriculture sector, where the weather is a dominant factor and the relationship between policy instruments and outcomes is so obviously tenuous.

Fifth, differences in interpretation arise when the initial conditions of the countries undergoing adjustment are not fully understood — such an understanding is critical.

Sixth, reform measures must be correctly identified for what they are. If, in the first phase of reform, the emphasis is on restructuring the budget and shifting the balance in the current account through expenditure reductions, it would be incorrect to call this a structural reform. These are stabilization measures, and their effects are very different from those of structural reforms. Several countries have called their stabilization efforts SAPs. The wrong labeling of adjustment, inaccurate grouping of adjusting countries, and incorrect choice of periods and duration of adjustment have been the most significant sources of confusion in this debate. Finally, one needs to know whether the reforms are implemented both in spirit and to the letter. Several countries have started adjustment programs and even borrowed from the international financial institutions but, under political pressure, have made reversals and slippages during the course of implementation. This stop–go approach has to be distinguished from a sustained implementation of planned reforms because reversals of policies benefit some segments of the population at the expense of others. For the World Bank, backsliding and failure to consistently implement its policies seem to be the main culprit.

In part, the controversies reflect differences in paradigms concerning the nature of the SAPs and what they should or should not do. Judging whether the SAPs are successes or failures and choosing which evaluation techniques to use hinge on one's philosophical view of how real markets operate and on one's perceptions of objectives, policy targets, and instruments. The word *adjustment* embraces too wide a range of policies and experiences to have one single meaning as an independent variable. It is, therefore, analytically and empirically difficult to link all the policy instruments to the ultimate targets (objectives) of policy. Analysts generally focus on whether a SAP has been effective in the sense of achieving its broad objectives. But even here there is little agreement about the methods of evaluation, the benchmark period, the time horizon over which a program could be said to have worked or not, the indices or variables for measuring performance, and the separation of the effects of the SAP per se from the effects of other factors.

Nevertheless, economists agree on several indicators of success. These include improvements in the rates of growth of GDP, revival of investments, and more efficient use of resources as revealed by increased productivity. The World Bank placed considerable value on these. Answering its own rhetorical question, "Is adjustment paying off in sub-Saharan Africa?," the World Bank (1994, p. 131) declared quite bluntly,

> The answer is a qualified yes. Adjustment programs may not have raised all countries' GDP growth, exports, savings and investment ratios to those of adjusting countries in other regions. But the stronger

reformers in Africa have turned around the decline in economic performance and are growing for the first time in many years.

In the several evaluation reports on adjustment written by World Bank staff (World Bank 1989a, 1989b, 1990, 1994; Elbadawi et al. 1992; Elbadawi and Uwujaren 1992; Hussain 1994; Hussain and Faruqee 1994), the evidence varies from report to report, but the World Bank as an institution maintains that adjustment is working. Although the reports have different emphases in terms of focus, a common methodological thread spans all of them. Other analysts obtain largely contradictory results, and the evaluation exercises differ markedly because of the techniques used. Besides the more fundamental points about problem articulation, choice of variables and time frame, country aggregation, and so forth, BWIs' staff and independent researchers have generally applied all kinds of performance-evaluation techniques.

Despite the disagreements about the techniques and results, there is an increasing sense of disappointment among the protagonists that the SAPs have not worked as expected in Africa. As Table 5 suggests, the patterns of economic growth and their levels reveal that adjustment has not made much of a difference. The World Bank (1994, pp. 1–2) regretted that after more than a decade of SAPs in Africa, "reforms remain incomplete," but the Bank attributed this not to the inefficacy or poor design of the SAPs but to "lack of implementation." It asserted that "no African country has achieved a sound macroeconomic policy stance, and there is considerable concern that the reforms undertaken to date are fragile and that they are merely returning Africa to the slow growth path of the 1960s and 1970s." It is unclear whether the lack of effective implementation results from unwillingness to undertake reforms; from the objective conditions of the economies not permitting the kind of adjustment being

Table 5. GDP growth under adjustment — agricultural-growth rate (median), sub-Saharan Africa, 1981–86 and 1987–91.

	GDP growth (%)	
	1981–86	1987–91
Large improvements	4.2	2.4
Small improvements	3.1	2.8
Deterioration	2.3	3.3
All countries	3.1	2.8

Source: ADB (1995).
Note: GDP, gross domestic product.

recommended; or from the policies being inherently nonimplementable. This debate has persisted since the initial controversies between UNECA and the World Bank. The bottom line, however, is that the SAPs have not delivered the promised recovery and growth, and several important gaps and weaknesses of the programs are increasingly being acknowledged.

Agriculture

What has been the result of such reforms on agriculture? In 1994, the World Bank's Chief Economist for the African region declared that "agriculture has been a particular success," although he conceded that the achievement has "been modest relative to external expectation" (Hussain 1994, p. 156). The World Bank (1994, p. 143) stated that these reforms "appear to have buoyed agricultural growth." It produced a table that suggested that those countries that had reduced the level of taxation enjoyed higher growth rates than those that had increased taxation. However, the World Bank (1994, pp. 143–146) also acknowledged that "no clear pattern emerged distinguishing countries in which macroeconomic policies deteriorated from those in which they did improve." The World Bank's explanation for these "not too surprising" results was the lags in other reforms, especially in marketing-board reforms and other government reforms.

The debate on the effect of SAPs on agriculture takes place in the context of a welter of conflicting data. For instance, although the World Bank data do tend to support its claims, those from the Food and Agriculture Organization of the United Nations and the African Development Bank (ADB) give a picture that is much less clear. Not only does the World Bank claim that its policies have led to recovery in agriculture, it even goes as far as to state that during 1988–92, Benin, Guinea, Mauritius, Nigeria, Tanzania, and Uganda each enjoyed an agricultural boom (World Bank 1995). The ADB (1995, p. 22) stated that "on average the reforms in agriculture, pursued by most African governments, have not had the rapid results in terms of increased output that were expected and a host of rigidities remains." Table 5 (ADB 1995) shows results that are substantially different from those of the World Bank. Before one makes much of these figures, one should recall once again that they are based on small samples from groups with wide variations of performance within each category. Therefore, not much significance should be attached to them. All in all, African agriculture's response to the SAPs has been what the World Bank (1994) euphemistically described as a disappointing performance. This compelled the World Bank (1994, p. 171) to ask, "What nonprice factors are still constraining the supply response: Does the sector have adequate capacity to adjust to changing incentives?" These are precisely the questions that various critics of SAPs have raised over the years.

The questions that immediately arise are these: What is behind the "disappointing performance?" To what could the few signs of recovery be accredited? Opinions differ sharply, partly because of differences in the data used. Here we advance a number of reasons that partly explain the failure despite considerable reform.

First, the objective of getting the prices right was far from adequate under the prevailing African conditions. The SAPs, by excessively focusing on prices, took attention away from problems of technological innovation, feebleness of commodity and financial markets, structural bottlenecks, the immense uncertainties created by the vagaries of capricious climate, and the many other constraints on agricultural transformation. The SAPs simply sidestepped all the major questions about the technical capacity of African agriculture to respond to price incentives and underestimated the many structural constraints binding African agriculture to low levels of productivity and responsiveness. Africa has yet to have its Green Revolution to cope with the demands of a rapid increase in population and the demands of high rates of urbanization. African agriculture lags far behind other developing countries in irrigation and fertilizer use and, consequently, crop yield. Only 4% of land is irrigated, compared with 26% in India and 44% in China. Similarly, fertilizer use is 8.9 kg/ha in Africa, whereas it is 68.7 kg/ha in India and 261.9 kg/ha in China. Agriculture in Africa is so dependent on weather that it is difficult to disentangle the effects of policy from those of exogenous factors such as rainfall. As the World Bank (1994) suggested with regard to Ghana and Nigeria, such structural factors as investment in research, rural infrastructure, global terms of trade, and marketing arrangements are also probably more important than prices.

Responsiveness to price incentives has been further blunted by a policy stance that has failed to address the decline in human-capital formation in the countryside (because of decreasing school-enrolment ratios) and the reduction in research, extension services, and rural infrastructure because of lower public expenditure. All these make the turnaround in agriculture a distant prospect.

Furthermore, part of the optimism about the efficacy of the SAPs and their objective of getting the prices right was based on assumptions about how wrong the prices actually faced by African farmers were. The fixation with prices was due to not only the assumption about the responsiveness of African farmers to price incentives but also the not always well-founded belief that African farmers were poorly rewarded for their efforts. Incongruously, this assumption is based on the belief that states, otherwise described as inefficient and impotent, can make official prices stick. However, the ubiquity of parallel markets in Africa has clearly demonstrated that the international financial institutions' fixation with official prices was misleading. In most countries, most agricultural products, especially those for the domestic markets, rarely passed through official channels. This is especially the case with foodstuffs whose prices were market determined, even in cases where the state had monopoly control of grain marketing. Food prices have been rising rapidly for more than two decades without provoking adequate supply response to keep pace with growth in populations and despite increased food imports.

Even for export crops, official prices have not always been the relevant ones. Azzam (1996, p. 143) reported that econometric studies in Côte d'Ivoire showed that parallel-market prices were more significant than the official ones, which seemed to play no part in the supply function; this led him to suppose that the prices effectively paid to the cocoa producers by the traders were more directly linked to international prices than to official prices:

> Under these conditions the reforms of the system of commercialisation and stabilisation of the prices of export products in Côte d'Ivoire should be considered less a problem of stimulating production than a problem of the distribution between the state and the producers of the margin between the price paid at the border and prices paid to producers.

African governments have gone a long way in reducing taxes on agricultural exports and in improving the terms of trade. Even with respect to prices, however, recent analyses indicate that in African economies external factors may account for the lion's share of the observed change in the domestic terms of trade for agriculture and taxable commodities. For example, Tshibaka (1998) observed that for Côte d'Ivoire, Nigeria, and Senegal as much as two-thirds of the change was accounted for by external factors. In other words, the gain from the removal of state monopsonies can easily be nullified by international terms-of-trade shifts.

Industrial performance

In an explicit response to those who have argued that the SAPs may be leading to deindustrialization, the World Bank (1994, p. 149) stated categorically that "industry is expanding." It argued that the impact of adjustment has been particularly marked in industrial and export growth. Its sample consisted of 29 countries in Africa that have had SAPs. Because many of these adjusting countries have not yet fully implemented the policy reforms recommended, the Bank divided them into three groups to assess the effects of SAPs : 6 with "large improvements" in macroeconomic policies, 9 with "small improvements," and 11 with "deterioration." Three were unclassified. Changes in growth performance, GDP, exports, industrial production, and agriculture were all assessed with reference to these categories and were separated into a preadjustment period (1981–86) and a postadjustment period (1987–91). The premises of the World Bank's argument are that the first group of countries shows the effects of structural adjustment the most; that the third group shows them the least; and, similarly, that the differences between the second period and the first show the effects of adjustment.

The effect of SAPs on manufacturing measured in this way showed that, on average, countries with the most adjustment have had the largest improvement in manufacturing performance; those with the least, the smallest. This purports to show that SAPs are good for industrial growth.

Although these findings appear to support a position pointing to the benefits of SAPs for industry, the statistical association between economic reforms (as defined by the three categories of policy change) and performance must be interpreted cautiously for the following reasons:

- The groupings according to improvements (large or small) and deterioration in policy have little or nothing to do with adjustment. They are based entirely on macroeconomic policies and not on adjustment in the sense of getting the prices right by import and other forms of liberalization. If they show anything, it is that improving internal and external balances is conducive to growth. The effect on resource allocation in response to market orientation cannot be assessed.
- Medians for groups have no statistical significance if individual variations within the groups are larger than the variations between groups.
- The group showing deterioration in policy had higher manufacturing growth rates in both periods than the other groups did;

the group showing large improvement had the lowest growth rate in the second period of adjustment. The conclusion could be that adjustment, as such, had no special effects on manufacturing growth and that the differences in growth rates were caused by other factors.

Adopting the grouping of countries given in *Adjustment in Africa* (World Bank 1994), Lall and Stewart (1996) showed that the relationship between industrial performance and policy improvement differs from that in the picture painted by the report. Various aspects of industrial performance in Africa were recalculated using more recent data from the ADB, as well as from the World Bank and other sources. The coverage was extended to 50 countries in Africa, including 21 that had not undergone adjustment (ADB 1995).

The periods used were also slightly different. A longer overall period, 1980–93, was taken; 1990–93 was used as the later subperiod to capture the more recent effects of policy reforms. The highest rate of growth in both periods was for the adjusting countries with improved macroeconomic policies. The lowest was for the countries in the group showing deterioration in policy in the 1980–93 period and for the nonadjusting low-income countries in the 1990–93 subperiod. This suggests, again, that macroeconomic-policy improvement helps economic growth in general; however, there is no significant statistical difference between any of the groups' growth rates. This indicates that the differences in group performance could be caused by factors other than macroeconomic-policy differences. The conclusion reached in *Adjustment in Africa* has not survived the test of time and greater coverage.

Although the expansion of exports has certainly been encouraging, it must be viewed from the context of starting with the very low performance base that typified the economic crisis period of the early to mid-1980s. The expansion rate has not been sustainable, and signs of stagnation have since appeared (1990–91). There was a significant decline in manufacturing exports and in nontraditional exports during 1990–94. The decline in nontraditional exports suggests that there is more to sustainable exporting than just eliminating "market distortions."

In the case of Ghana, the story is similar. MVA did rise rapidly after 1983, when imported inputs were made available to existing industries that were suffering from substantial excess capacity (Figure 4). However, as liberalization spread to other imports and excess capacity was used up, the exposure to world competition led to a steady deceleration of

Figure 4. Growth in manufacturing value added in Ghana, 1967–94.

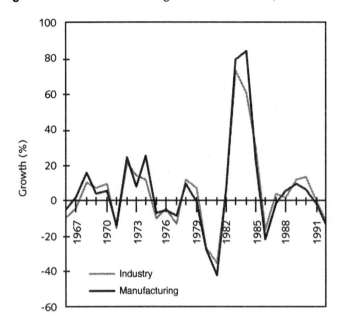

industrial growth. Thus, the MVA growth rate fell to 5.1% in 1988, 5.6% in 1989, 1.1% in 1990, 2.6% in 1991, and 1.1% in 1992.

The case of Ghana warrants special attention because this country has been used to indicate the benefits of far-reaching adjustment sustained over time. According to the World Bank (1994), one of the effects of adjustment has been the revival of Ghana's industry. Indeed, in the Bank's comparison of degrees of adjustment, Ghana — which is classified as one of the countries with large improvements in macroeconomic policies — enjoyed a fairly impressive improvement in average growth rate of manufacturing, from –0.4% in 1981–86 to 4.5% in 1987–91. What these figures do not reveal is the one-off character of the gains, a point brought out sharply when we plot the MVA growth rates over several years. What emerges is that the increase in output was due not so much to liberalization as to relaxation of constraints on capacity use as a result of increased inflow of aid to bring in intermediate goods. Once the excess capacity was used and once industry was exposed to world competition, industrial growth decelerated.

Such performance cannot be taken seriously and does not suggest that Ghanaian manufacturing is responding well to liberalization. Employment in manufacturing fell from a peak of 78 700 in 1987 to 28 000 in 1993 (ADB 1994). The number of small enterprises has risen, but these are in low-productivity activities aimed at local markets. Foreign investment has not responded well to the adjustment — most of it is concentrated in primary activities, rather than in manufacturing — and domestic private investment has not picked up sufficiently to boost the manufacturing sector. The World Bank survey (1996, p. 38), noting that downsizing is "troublesome," ventured to make the following comment, although it includes a question peremptorily dismissed in the earlier (1994) publication:

> With policy reforms in progress in all the countries involved in our investigation, one would expect to observe more than the normal amount of adjustment activity. The question is whether it is excessive to the point where productive resources are being forced out of manufacturing and into lower value activities in other sectors of the economy.

Privatization

Privatization was the centrepiece of anything resembling industrial policy in the SAPs. Over the years, liberalization has increasingly meant privatization. In *Adjustment in Africa*, the World Bank (1994) admitted that the efforts to privatize state corporations and to improve their performance have yielded meager results. The Bank blamed this on the resistance of African governments to privatization. This is not exactly fair. The private sector has not, in general, responded well in terms of investments. Also, most problems of privatization are related to the overall failure to stimulate both domestic and foreign private investment. In many cases, there simply have been no stakers and no private investors willing to buy and manage state enterprises. Privatization has also been based on the assumption that investors with adequate financial resources do exist and that they simply are waiting for governments to get out of the way. The poor response to what is obviously an improved climate belies this perception of the nature of the private sector in Africa and the responses of foreign private capital to the privatization initiative. Quite obviously, serious privatization should have been accompanied by a series of microlevel interventionist policies to support the private sector.

One reason for the failure of privatization to yield the expected results is that privatization has thus far taken a rather ad hoc form. This is largely because it has been carried out in response to fiscal crises, balance-of-payments problems, and external pressure, especially from the BWIs. It has not been part of a systematic strategy to restructure the role of the state and promote the private sector in accordance with some perception of the long-term developmental exigencies of the economy. Consequently, it has failed to have the credibility needed to elicit the necessary response from the private sector. Seen as a long-term strategy of capitalist development, privatization would obviously not have been accompanied by a laissez-faire view of the role of the state.

It should also be noted that privatization is, after all, a state policy to be implemented by the state. The state must in most cases fund the privatization process. Here one should bear in mind that most governments in Africa simply had no fiscal capacity to "fatten the calves" before selling them. In addition, the state must manage and administer the process of privatization. The weakening of the state's administrative capacity does not facilitate privatization. In most cases, it leads to privatization of state assets without the state's express approval through what is tantamount to cannibalizing the state without increasing output or productivity in the privatized enterprises. Also, where such privatization takes place within an essentially monopolistic market, the promised efficiency gains may not be forthcoming.

Technology

Before leaving the question of the SAPs and industry it is necessary to touch briefly on the question of technology, which is conspicuous by its absence in *Adjustment in Africa* (World Bank 1994).

The orthodox view is that price distortion has led to the wrong choice of technologies in Africa. Correction of prices would lead to a more appropriate choice. Experience elsewhere confirms that technological acquisition and innovation are a public good that demands more explicit policies by the state than are allowed for in the SAPs. The downsizing and closure of factories have in many cases led to waste of scarce skilled human resources.

Moreover, the absence of clearly spelled out measures to enhance Africa's capacity to move up the technological ladder is linked to the death of industrial policy or a vision of African economies doing more than exporting primary commodities. However, even that task requires some technical skills for research and management.

Trade

In an evaluation of the effect of trade liberalization, the typical target variables include changes in output, in various components of trade, in the performance of the manufacturing sector, and in employment. As noted earlier, many African countries have embarked on a sharp shift in their trade policies. Exchange rates have been devalued or left to find their "true" market value. Tariff rates have been slashed, and quantitative restrictions on imports have been relaxed or removed altogether. Reforms in the exchange rate were geared toward shifting resources to the more productive sectors and stimulating exports, but trade liberalization has meant that clients have options to import many items.

One of the expectations of trade policy was that it would not only lead to an increase in Africa's traditional exports but also eventually encourage the expansion of nontraditional exports, especially in simple manufactures. Some of the sample countries used by the World Bank (1994) recorded some export recovery, but it could not be sustained. The initial recovery was a temporary phenomenon that was followed by a decline. This outcome was demonstrated by the cases of Ghana and Tanzania — countries that have been categorized as relatively successful adjusters (World Bank 1994). For instance, in Tanzania, devaluation accompanied by resumption of foreign-aid inflow induced some output recovery and export expansion largely from the industries that experienced output recovery. Much of this output recovery originated from better use of existing capacities, rather than from new investments.

A few summarizing generalizations can be made on the basis of the trade-liberalization experiences of a set of countries (see Oyejide 1998):

- Resources have shifted away from the import-substituting and nontradable sectors to the tradable ones. As a result, exports have responded positively, although modestly, and trade shares have generally increased.
- Some deindustrialization has occurred in some countries. Trade liberalization has unleashed competitive pressures that many previously sheltered and inefficient industrial firms have been unable to cope with. Yet, new export-oriented activities have not increased sufficiently to take up the slack.
- Trade-policy changes have not led to any noticeable diversification of exports. More specifically, there has been virtually no increase

in the exports of manufactured goods (Oyejide 1996; Wangwe and Semboja 1998; see also Table 6).

Until quite recently, African countries faced unfavourable trade conditions as terms of trade declined. Recent improvements in some key commodity prices may once again push African countries to intensify their export of primary products. However, one should bear in mind that available empirical evidence on the terms of trade in SSA seems to prove that the basis for the export-pessimism thesis continues to hold. A World Bank study, taking the year 1980 as the base, indicated that the terms-of-trade index declined to 91 in 1985 and 84 in 1987 (World Bank 1989a). In a more general survey of empirical studies on this subject, Killick (1992) concluded that the thesis of the declining real commodity price was then more widely accepted than before.

Recent efforts to revive exports within the traditional setting have provided further evidence that exports cannot provide an engine for growth unless the export structure changes. Evaluating the impact of SAPs in SSA, Hussain (1994) indicated that between 1985 and 1990, the export volumes of nine major export commodities in countries that had under-taken adjustment programs increased by 75% over the 1977–79 averages. Yet (and most interestingly), export earnings from these exports fell by 40% over the same period because of deteriorating barter terms of trade (Hussain 1994).

Two factors account for the failure of export diversification. First, an industrial policy to turn some of the existing industries into export industries was absent. Liberalization in Africa moved at a much faster pace than in Asia and too fast to allow for orderly industrial restructuring.

Table 6. Pre- and post-adjustment manufactured exports.

	Burkina	Ghana	Tanzania	Uganda	Zimbabwe
Exports					
Preadjustment (million USD)	15.7	5.3	43.9	1.2	428.7
Most recent (million USD)	17.3	10.4	61.9	0.5	387.9
Change (%)	10.2	103.9	41.0	−58.3	−9.5
Share in total exports					
Preadjustment (%)	12.1	0.7	14.4	0.3	30.8
Most recent (%)	12.1	1.1	15.7	0.3	31.3
Change (%)	0.0	0.4	1.3	0.0	0.5

Source: Engberg-Pedersen et al. (1996).
Note: USD, United States dollars.

The abruptness of the liberalization process did not provide enough time for the investment in capital and human resources needed to reshape the orientation of the industry. Second (and a corollary to this) a clear investment–export nexus to exploit the more favourable price structure for new export activities was nonexistent. Furthermore, continued credibility of some of the trade-liberalization processes will be seriously challenged, as the heavy reliance on external financing may be unsustainable.

Financial-resource mobilization

One expectation among most Africans was that financial liberalization and the BWIs' stamp of approval would increase domestic savings and, by opening access to private banks and financial institutions, attract direct investment. Such expectations have thus far not been fulfilled.

DOMESTIC SAVINGS AND FINANCIAL-SECTOR LIBERALIZATION

Perhaps the most fateful failure of adjustment in terms of long-term growth has been in resource mobilization. Domestic savings and investments have been extremely low, even in the success stories. The mean savings ratio was only 10% for "strong adjusters," and, among these, most had savings below this average. Interestingly, the mean for the countries with deteriorating policy stance was 13%. One should compare these rates with those of Asian countries to understand the tasks ahead.

The World Bank (1994) report devoted a section to financial-sector reform. The report considered the exercise less successful than the reforms in trade and agriculture and macroeconomic stabilization. The dashed expectations for the financial-sector reforms were attributed to the failure of real interest to remain consistently positive over the reform period — a result of high fiscal deficits. The report further noted that the public sector still controlled a large share of bank credits and interfered in the management of the financial sector. The report attributed the poor performance of the reform to inappropriate sequencing; state interference in the management of financial systems; and weak regulatory and supervisory capacity and institutions. Based on this, the report recommended further efforts to reduce financial repression, restore bank solvency, and improve financial infrastructure.

In line with the McKinnon–Shaw hypothesis, the reforms aimed at achieving positive and rising real interest rates to raise the level of real financial savings. It was assumed that real savings is interest elastic. Although this is known to hold unquestionably in developed countries, it is hardly the case in African countries, where the relationship is either weak or nonexistent (ADB 1995). The results of the reforms support this argument. Except for the few African countries that experienced massive capital inflow, most had decreased real investment.

Most empirical work suggests that interest rates have no significant role in determining financial or total savings in Africa. Real income is found to be the most important determinant of total savings, whereas the activity of the informal market is found to be the most important determinant of financial savings.

These findings were corroborated by Giovanni (1983), Mwega et al. (1992), and Nissanke (1994) for other developing countries. Manipulation of the real interest rate is clearly not a reliable policy instrument for mobilizing resources in the context of African countries. Both total and financial savings are unresponsive to movements in the real interest rate, and its effect on investment is uncertain.

Even if it is admitted that financial liberalization does not lead to an overall increase in savings, it is argued that by bringing together savers and investors, financial markets in a competitive setting can improve the allocative efficiency of the economy. One should, however, remember the assumptions about the existence and performance of markets underlying such an assertion. One of the major implications of the market-failure approach is that financial deregulation does not necessarily improve the allocative efficiency of the economy because it cannot remove the distortions related to equilibrium credit rationing and other noncompetitive behaviour of financial institutions, although it could lessen the distortions caused by government intervention.

The high nominal interest rates that resulted from the reforms — as well as the asymmetry of information in these financial markets, moral hazard, and adverse selection that ensued — contributed to the increased fragility and distress of the financial systems. Although these problems have been recognized in the literature (Stiglitz 1989, 1993), the World Bank (1994) report chose to ignore it, focusing only on the repressed-interest-rate paradigm.

The magnitude of these problems could have been less if the reforms had been implemented gradually and in pace with fiscal reforms and the carrying capacity of the financial infrastructure (including the regulatory and supervisory roles of government), as Ghana has exemplified. The undue haste in implementing the reforms can partly be understood in terms of the pressure from the international donors (particularly the World

Bank and the IMF) that, in the first instance, led Africa in the reform direction. The ownership of the reforms, including the haste of implementation, goes to these external institutions. The contributions of Africa were either in not keeping faith with the urge to push harder when the expected results were not forthcoming or in not embarking on all the measures in the reform package, as typified by Nigeria.

Furthermore, given the small size of the formal financial sector in Africa, the low income level, and the lack of a savings base that can be mobilized through improved real savings, the continent needs to have modest and cautious expectations for the gains to be made from the improved price of savings and a healthy financial sector. The concentration on banking has yielded mixed results for the banking sector itself. Although it has led to an increase in the number and varieties of banking and other financial institutions, there have been no improvements in the maturity structure of deposit liabilities of banks and nonbanks, leading to asset–liability mismatch. In Nigeria, the bulk of the credit that was channeled to the private sector was mainly directed toward short-term investment. Between 1987 and 1994, 50% of the private-sector credits went to call money; 32.5%, to loans maturing within 12 months; 12%, to loans maturing within 1–5 years (medium-term); and only 4.8%, to long-term investments exceeding 5 years (Inanga and Ekpenyong 1998). In other words, long-term investment, which is one of the fundamentals for development, is not being stimulated. In addition, these reforms have not brought any improvement in the access to credit by small- and medium-scale enterprises (SMEs) and rural dwellers.

In implementing the reforms, African countries failed to take the peculiarities of their financial structures and economies into account. The rural–urban dichotomy, the needs of SMEs, and the role of the large informal sector were ignored (ADB 1994).

FOREIGN CAPITAL

If higher interest rates did not lead to increases in total domestic savings partly because of low levels of income, it was expected that the rates would attract foreign investment by compensating for higher risks and foreign-exchange instability.

Thus far, response to Africa's SAPs and "getting the fundamentals right" has not paid any dividends. As Table 7 shows, of the more than 112 billion USD lent to the developing countries in 1995, only about 5.7 billion USD went to SSA.

Table 7. Flow of capital to developing countries, 1994–96.

	Flow of capital (million USD)				
				1996	
	1994	1995	Q_1	Q_2	Q_3
All developing countries	72 780	112 358	24 249	21 944	21 444
Private	32 110	58 965	14 351	16 006	13 138
Sub-Saharan Africa	1 022	2 606	815	2 144	446
East Asia and Pacific	20 685	36 337	11 139	10 056	9 596
South Asia	1 857	2 400	643	171	304
Europe and Central Asia	1 645	5 344	816	1 125	1 089
Latin America	6 434	11 621	938	2 255	1 669
Middle East and North Africa	467	657	0	255	915
Sovereign	10 604	7 284	1 123	678	915
Sub-Saharan Africa	28	411	40	0	375
East Asia and Pacific	4 074	1 727	98	542	100
South Asia	283	361	375	0	182
Europe and Central Asia	2 585	1 666	60	136	108
Latin America	585	2 914	350	0	0
Middle East and North Africa	3 048	205	200	0	150
Other public	30 066	46 109	8 775	5 260	7 390
Sub-Saharan Africa	311	2 649	440	185	349
East Asia and Pacific	14 568	19 634	3 024	1819	2 310
South Asia	2 411	3 339	968	1 082	720
Europe and Central Asia	6 692	6 759	2 845	994	2 374
Latin America	4 838	5 660	937	1 079	1 627
Middle East and North Africa	1 246	8 067	561	100	10

Source: Computed from Euromoney Loanware and World Bank.
Note: Q_1, Q_2, Q_3, first to third quarters; USD, United States dollars.

This perhaps should not come as a surprise. Growing theoretical and empirical evidence suggests that owing to the segmentation in global markets, certain regions may not benefit from capital movements. The region invariably cited is SSA. One can distinguish two sets of factors that may induce capital to move to any particular country: the "push factors" in a capital-exporting country and the "pull factors" in a capital-receiving country. The push factors include the rates of return in the capital-exporting countries: low interests rates push investors into the world market in search of lucrative investment opportunities. The pull factors include high rates of returns and financial stability in the capital-importing country.

The financial liberalization accompanying adjustment programs pursued in Africa is based on a pull theory, which suggests that African countries, by improving their creditworthiness (through adhering to SAPs and receiving the stamp of approval of BWIs), can tilt the flow of capital in their favour. This view has been challenged. For one thing, it is doubtful that creditworthiness indicators reflect domestic factors. Fernandez (1993) showed both theoretically and empirically that external factors, especially international interest rates, have a substantial effect on a country's creditworthiness:

> The key importance of country creditworthiness is confirmed by the experience of low creditworthiness countries where the surge did not materialize, such as sub-Saharan African countries. For them, improvements in country creditworthiness have not been large enough to lead to levels exceeding the credit rationing threshold.

> To a large extent, developing country creditworthiness has been in turn driven by external factors, especially international interest rates. The previous finding on the importance of improvements in country creditworthiness is best seen as a channel through which underlying factors, external factors for the most part, induced capital inflows.

Fernandez's (1993, p. 414) conclusions are worth citing at length:

> In terms of causal underlying factors, the surge of capital inflows in most countries appears to have been largely pushed by low returns in developed countries, both directly or through the country credit-worthiness channel, as opposed to pulled by domestic factors. Even if domestic conditions in middle-income countries had remained unchanged we could have witnessed a massive and widespread surge of capital inflows driven by the quite favourable evolution of external factors. There are important country exceptions, namely Argentina, Korea, and most notably, Mexico, but in most countries no surge in inflows would have taken place in the absence of remarkable reductions in international interest rates.

> Consequently, most developing countries are vulnerable to adverse exogenous developments that would render capital unsustainable. Capital inflows in the typical country are largely dependent on favourable international interest rates and, ceteris paribus, would not be sustained if they return to higher levels.

One should not forget that indices such as "country default risk" are highly subjective. Asymmetric information and agency problems in global financial markets mean that high rates of return on securities do not compensate for risk — real or imagined — and lead to credit rationing that can freeze out whole countries. Indeed, if a country's creditworthiness is too low, then capital is rationed; the involuntary flows that then emerge from negotiations occur in large part independently of the specifics of return profiles.

Various studies clearly suggest that African economies provide higher returns to investors than any other developing region (UNCTAD 1995). Yet, for all this, Africa did not attract much foreign direct investment (FDI). The explanation given for this poor response is risk, at least as perceived by investors. The point here is that African initiatives are unlikely to make the most important difference in the creditworthiness of the continent.

A dramatic change has occurred in the 1990s in the financial flows to developing countries. In 1993, the net transfer to developing countries rose to 48 billion USD. Nearly half of this (20 billion USD) went to Latin America. Africa was off the map for such transactions. In more recent years, some hints have been given that Africa's turn is coming. One should, however, bear in mind a number of issues. Flows of finance do not necessarily correspond to flows of real investment. In addition, the high correlation between domestic savings and investments challenges the claims that the integration of international markets has created a market where flows of savings and investment know no national boundaries. Most of the flows to emerging markets have been extremely volatile. As Oshikoya and Ogbu (1998) observed, most of the flows into Africa's emerging market have been in highly speculative activities. The high degree of volatility of such flows adds to the instability of the economies, and, arguing further, Oshikoya and Ogbu maintained that this considerable uncertainty could make share prices and stock markets much less useful as guides to the allocation of resources.

Human resources

We noted that the World Bank's view on education has been essentially informed by ROREs and that this has had implications for resource allocation to and within the education sector itself. The basis of the Bank's policy conclusions has been challenged by both African policymakers and academics on several points.

First, the empirical basis for these far-reaching conclusions is poor, according to Bennell (1996). Bennell has demonstrated, for instance, that the evidence used by the World Bank is ambiguous: only in 4 of 12 countries did differences between primary and secondary rates exceed 2%.

Appleton and Mackinnon (1996) cited evidence from Côte d'Ivoire, Ethiopia, Ghana, Kenya, South Africa, and Uganda that tends to indicate that wage returns for secondary schooling are fairly high, whereas those for primary schooling are low. In other words, we are, empirically, in murky waters, and the pronouncements and reforms that the World Bank has made with so much certitude are on shaky ground.

Second, the analysis has tended to be rather static. ROREs calculated for one period may not be valid under different economic conditions. It is interesting to note that the ROREs for primary education have fallen during the crisis. A policy on human-capital formation based on these cyclical rates of return would produce the kind of tragic situations in Africa in which educational institutions have been starved of funding because of their apparent low rates of return as measured at a particular point in the cycle. The rate-of-return analysis is quite a blunt instrument for decisions about outcomes so dependent on rate of growth, the structural transformation of the economy, and technological change.

Furthermore, both the absence of an industrial policy and the heavy leaning toward Africa's historical comparative advantage in primary-product exports have tended to obviate the need for high-level skilled human resources in Africa, which partly accounts for the suggestion that rates of returns of higher education are low in Africa. Such an argument on rates of return can only make sense in the absence of any long-term vision of technological development within the state and within that particular logic of comparative advantage in primary commodities.

SAPs and poverty

One of the widely accepted fundamentals of development is the alleviation of poverty. Development-focused adjustment would include this as one of its key indicators in both the short-term and the long-term views. The proponents of the SAPs have tended to maintain two, not exactly compatible, positions:

- That while going through "the vale of tears," African countries will have to accept increases in poverty, especially among groups that benefited from the pre-SAP policy regime; and
- That by favouring the rural and informal sectors and by "leveling the playing field," the SAPs will improve the incomes of the poor.

Such views partly explain why SAPs have tended to append poverty considerations as an afterthought — poverty reduction was not an explicit central objective of early adjustment programs (World Bank 1994). This also accounts for the complacency often induced by the ideological assumption that the SAPs would automatically help the poor.

Following the special attention drawn to issues of poverty by popular protests, by African governments, and more dramatically by the United Nations Children's Fund, the World Bank became a major contributor in the SAPs–poverty debate. An immense research program on poverty has developed within the World Bank, and numerous journal articles on the program's results have been published. This massive research output, which includes theoretical contributions, model simulations, and empirical studies, seems to have been directed to proving that adjustment programs did not hurt the poor in Africa and that more, rather than less, adjustment is needed for poverty reduction.

In *Adjustment in Africa*, the World Bank (1994, p. 163) addressed the issue in a more direct fashion. According to the World Bank, the SAPs have

> often been accused of hurting the poor. To address this issue, it is useful to focus on two questions: would the poor have benefited from less adjustment? And, to the extent that adjustment benefited the poor, could policy reforms have been designed differently to have benefited them more?

The method used to answer these questions was indirect: it was noted (World Bank 1994, p. 163) that adjustment

> has contributed to faster GDP per-capita growth in half of the countries examined, and there is every reason to think that it has helped the poor, based on the strong linkages between growth and poverty reduction elsewhere in the world.

Thus, no evidence was provided on causality.

One of the questions posed by the World Bank (1994) was "What has happened to the indicators of poverty in Africa over the last five years?" Lack of appropriate information, however, precluded the possibility of a definitive answer to the question. On the basis of preliminary results from seven countries, the World Bank (1994) concluded that recent analysis of poverty and social indicators suggests that, along with growth, the pattern of growth is important and called for a decomposition of the change in poverty into a growth component and a distribution component. One should, however, note that the World Bank (1994, p. 165) has been compelled by the evidence to adopt a more cautious position, arguing that "adjustment-led growth has probably helped the poor."

In another World Bank study on SAPs and poverty, Demery and Squire (1996) set out to provide "the most convincing evidence to date that economic reform is consistent with a decline in overall poverty and that a failure to reform is associated with increased poverty." Claiming their analysis was "solidly grounded" and based on the recently available data from household surveys for six SSA countries at two points in time, they dismissed earlier contributions, which used to be quoted by the World Bank in support of its unrelenting enforcement of SAPs in SSA countries, as having been theoretical (or having used indirect evidence based on modeling exercises) or having relied on anecdotal evidence.

In a study by Ali (1998), which used data from the International Fund for Agricultural Development (IFAD) and classified countries according to the World Bank's categories, 10 SSA countries were classified as "intensively adjusting" (Ghana, Kenya, Malawi, Tanzania, and Zambia), "other adjusting" (Gabon, Gambia, and Mali), or "nonadjusting" (Ethiopia and Lesotho). For each of the 10 countries, IFAD had reported the head-count ratio as a measure of poverty for 1965–88.

For the intensively adjusting countries, it was found that the index of rural poverty had increased from 56.6% in 1965 to 62.4% in 1988. Similarly, for the other adjusting countries, the index of rural poverty increased from 45.1% in 1965 to 60.7% in 1988. The corresponding absolute number of the poor increased from 18.2 million to 36.2 million for the intensively adjusting group and from 2.3 million to 5.1 million for the other adjusting group. In contrast, the head-count ratio for the non-adjusting group decreased from 65.8% in 1965 to 43.6% in 1988, and the absolute number of the poor remained constant around 17 million.

Table 8 shows that three countries recorded a large improvement in policies (reflected by a score of >1 for an overall change in macroeconomic policies). In all three, however, poverty increased. In Ghana, the best-performing country in terms of policy, poverty increased by 4.49 percentage points (in absolute terms) between 1985 and 1990, an increase of 15.5%, the fourth largest increase among the 10 countries in the sample. Tanzania, the country performing the second best in terms of policy, saw poverty increase by 6.26 percentage points between 1985 and 1990: this was an increase of 11.7%, the fifth lowest increase. In Zimbabwe, the country performing the third best in terms of policy, poverty increased by the highest absolute number, 10.55 percentage points, which was the third highest increase, at 18.6%.

Table 8. Structural-adjustment programs and poverty in sub-Saharan Africa, 1985 and 1990.

	Head-count ratio (%) 1985	1990	Change in poverty (% points)	Change in macroeconomic policy (score)
Côte d'Ivoire	40.31	45.93	5.62	–1.3
Ghana	29.00	33.49	4.49	2.2
Kenya	53.17	58.83	5.66	0.5
Mauritania	32.17	35.52	3.35	0.5
Rwanda	31.59	37.94	6.35	–0.2
Senegal	49.65	54.75	5.10	0.5
Tanzania	53.53	59.79	6.26	1.5
Uganda	37.10	44.69	7.59	0.2
Zambia	48.53	52.54	4.01	–0.3
Zimbabwe	56.71	67.26	10.55	1.0

Source: Ali (1998).

At the other end of the scale, we have three countries recording deterioration in policy. The worst-performing country in terms of policy was Côte d'Ivoire, where poverty increased by 5.62 percentage points, which was the fifth highest increase, at 13.9%. The country performing the second worst in terms of policy was Zambia, where the increase in poverty was second lowest in absolute terms (4.01 percentage points), giving the lowest increase in poverty, at 8.3%. Rwanda was the country performing the third worst in terms of policy, and poverty increased there by 6.35 percentage points, giving the second highest increase in poverty, at 20.1%.

Nobody in his or her right senses would argue that "sound macro-economic policies" and "sound economic growth" will not reduce poverty. However, surely reasonable men and women can disagree on the definition of the adjective *sound* as it applies to policies and to growth. There are differences between poverty-reducing growth paths and other growth paths (see, for example, World Bank 1995). Whether, in fact, the SAP is a growth-inducing strategy is questionable in its own right. It is even more questionable whether the SAP is a poverty-reducing growth path.

Adding to the ranks of the poor, who are still mainly rural, are the urban poor. In reality, the urban workers have been conspicuously the most adversely affected social group. The overall effects of the SAPs on urban workers have been dramatic declines in real wages, increased unemployment, and deteriorating employment conditions (greater informalization and instability of employment). For instance, in Côte d'Ivoire, the real per capita income of urban workers declined by more than 20% during the adjustment period. Employment dropped by as much as 85% in the building sector. This was not only an expected outcome but a desired one, at least in the short run. It was one of the tenets of new liberalism that labour markets in Africa were highly distorted by minimum-wage and job-security legislation that made the labour markets inflexible. Stabilization generally aims at reducing real wages, partly to reduce aggregate demand and partly to cheapen labour costs. And in Africa, wages have declined sharply. The World Bank (1995, p. 104) stated the case as follows:

> Labour does tend to suffer during the initial period of adjustment, and possibly more than capital. But most often it is not because the design of the adjustment policies is flawed, but because adjustment occurs simultaneously with — or is triggered by — a macroeconomic crisis, followed by a sharp drop in aggregate demand. Labour is less internationally mobile than capital and thus less able to leave when the domestic economy declines. So when an economy crashes labour is likely to bear the brunt of the shock, while capital flees. But it is usually the aggregate demand shock, not the ensuing adjustment that hurts labour.

Presumably, the fall in real wages was accepted on the premise that this would lead to more employment: first, through output expansion attendant upon redistribution of income in favour of capitalists; and second, through adoption of more labour-absorbing technologies because, by doing away with "financial repression," the SAP would produce interest rates that induce adoption of technologies reflective of a country's factor endowment. This would provide employment opportunities for the poor, especially in the so-called informal sector (McKinnon 1973). This has not taken place in Africa. Declining real wages have not been associated with declining unemployment. In the 14 countries for which relevant data are available, the annual growth rate in formal-sector employment fell from 2.8% in the 1975–80 period to 1% in the 1980s. The sector targeted by the SAPs has been the public sector, along with the parastatal subsectors. Retrenchment in the civil service has played an important part in swelling the ranks of the poor. The World Bank's (1994, p. 170) response to all this is "not to worry":

> The layoffs of public sector employees, who are those hardest hit by adjustment, have not generally added to the number of poor people. Many of those who lost their jobs were able to find other work, often by returning to rural areas.

Moreover, increased labour-market "flexibility" has not increased employment in the formal sector. One explanation may once again be the earlier exaggeration of labour-market distortions. As the ILO (1996) observed,

> It should be noted that the actual effect of minimum wage laws on the functioning of labour markets depends not only on the level but also on how effectively the laws are enforced in each country. Studies have found that in many developing countries where a minimum wage law exists it is not always effectively enforced. This is shown by the large number of workers earning below the legal minimum rate in these countries. Empirical evidence seems to suggest that countries rarely set minimum wages at levels that cut seriously into employment. One explanation for this is offered by Freeman, who posits that countries follow a strategy of "optimal selective enforcement" of minimum wage (and other) regulations; that is, they effectively implement these laws when the cost is modest in terms of lost jobs, but they enforce the laws weakly when the cost of employment is sizeable. Low minimum wages and lax enforcement thus seriously undermine the validity of the "distortionary" view of minimum wages.

Social programs

Mounting a research offensive on poverty, the World Bank has introduced programs to alleviate the problems caused by the crisis and adjustment programs. These have generally been uneasily tacked onto the SAPs as an afterthought or as a preemptive measure in response to expected political troubles. The overwhelming evidence is that these programs have performed poorly (Ewonkem 1996; Ogwumike 1998). This is partly because of the limited financial resources allocated to them compared to the overall funding for the SAPs. Poor performance is also inherent to measures intended to solve problems within a model that denies the emergence of those problems. Finally, the high political profile given to these programs has compromised their efficacy, as funds are thinly spread to cover as wide a range as possible (Stewart 1995; Vivian 1995).

Poverty elimination, therefore, was not one of the areas of key focus in the adjustment program. Grudgingly, the World Bank (1994) conceded that its programs had not really addressed the issue of poverty. The initial response of international financial institutions was something like this: an increase in poverty cannot happen under the SAPs; however, as it is happening, remedial measures should be introduced. One effect of such an approach is that programs to mitigate the negative effects of the SAPs have simply been pasted onto the SAPs in an ad hoc manner without "problematizing" (let alone challenging) the core assumptions and policies of the programs that may have spawned the ills that the measures were supposed to redress. That these measures did not challenge the core SAP model was underlined by the fact that they were explicitly given the additional objective of drumming up political support for the SAPs. Consequently, the donors insisted on the high visibility of such programs to counter the political opposition to the SAPs.

Governance and state capacity

The SAPs have been undertaken simultaneously with political liberalization in Africa. Considerable debate has arisen over the causal relationship between these two streams of liberalization. One group argues that opposition to the SAPs mobilized large sections of the population against the authoritarian rule identified with both the crisis and adoption of the SAPs. Others argue that greater economic liberalization weakened the hold of the state and opened space for independent social and political action, leading to calls for democratization. Still others argue that the external pressures stemming from globalization on the economic front and from donor political conditionalities precipitated these changes. Whatever the real reason, these twin processes have been unleashed in Africa, and the question is how these processes interact to reinforce or undermine each other. More significantly, to what extent do the SAPs enhance the process of democratization in Africa?

Structural adjustment has affected democratization on at least three levels. At the first level, the effects of SAPs relate to a growing private space, signified by greater visibility of civil society. This has persuaded some to see SAPs as essential components of democratization in Africa. One should note, however, that the private space created by the SAPs is not all enabling or empowering. Much of this space increasingly manifests as the informalization of economic life and marginalization of large sections of the population, eventually detaching them from any formal political organization.

At the second level, the SAPs have affected the legitimacy of new governments. The adjustment years have been marked by a further erosion of the legitimacy of the postcolonial African state, with implications for its political capacity to implement policies. The efforts to retrench the state not only helped to curb its social reach but also further undermined the postcolonial social contract, on the basis of which the state sought to construct ideological legitimation, build political alliances, relate with the opposition, and secure the cooperation or support of autonomous centres of power (Olukoshi and Laakso 1996).

At the third level, SAPs have affected the process of policy-making. The packaging and conditionalities of the SAPs appear to be imposed and leave little room for choice and negotiation at the national level.

Administrative incapacitation

The crisis and adjustment years in Africa have had far-reaching, adverse consequences for the administrative structure and capacity of many countries on the continent. The governance program of the donors has hardly addressed these consequences in a manner that supports meaningful renewal. Many civil-service organizations have been severely weakened not only by staff retrenchments and the effects of the exercises on the morale of those retained but also by the collapse of the income (and purchasing power) of public-sector employees as a result of currency devaluation and massive inflationary pressures.

Even where the sharp decline in the real value of civil-service pay was already under way during the preadjustment period, it was reinforced by the devaluation measures that became the defining feature of the quest for adjustment and the inflationary pressures associated with this. In many countries, wage and salary freezes were also imposed; several countries even cut the nominal pay of their civil servants. From being competitive with the remuneration available to employees in the local private sector, civil-service pay in most African countries during the adjustment years fell way behind; it became even less competitive internationally. As one consequence of this, experienced and qualified personnel have been draining out of the public sector, partly into the local private sector but overwhelmingly into the international labour market.

Without doubt, in most countries, the civil service needed overhauling, and retrenchment may have been necessary. However, the way it has been carried out testifies more to an ideological bias against big government than to any mere rationalization of an inefficient and bloated bureaucracy. In most cases, reforms have been guided by a simple rule of thumb without a full understanding of either the quantities or the qualities involved.

It is important to underline the collapse of wages and salaries in the public sector because this has been central to the decrease in public-sector morale and effectiveness. In a sense, the wholesale, one-sided antistatist ideology on which the neoliberal reform project for Africa was inaugurated cast the civil service in a bad light, so the overall emphasis of the World Bank's reform effort was on cutting it down to size. The centrality of the stabilization-programs' goal of restoring internal fiscal balances left the state little room to seriously consider ways to enhance the pay and purchasing power of civil servants. Thus, the antistatism of the adjustment packages both reinforced and was reinforced by the demand-management and deflationary thrust of the economic-reform programs. The focus of attention was, therefore, on cost containment or reduction that almost always translated into pay freezes and the retrenchment of workers.

Of course, some people suggested that the savings from the reduction in the size of the civil service might be used to enhance the pay of those who remained in public-sector employment. However, this was more an ideological proposition for legitimating retrenchment than a serious proposal for pay review with a view to making the civil service an attractive place to make a career. Not surprisingly, the proposal never gathered steam anywhere in Africa, and any efforts to make the civil service more professional, efficient, and effective have been undermined by the very adjustment package on the basis of which reform is pursued.

Faced with diminishing real incomes (and purchasing power) and ever-rising costs of living, many public-sector employees have resorted to moonlighting activities and abuse of state property. It is not surprising that the civil service all over Africa has found it increasingly difficult to attract and retain high-calibre local personnel with the requisite experience and expertise. Governments have largely been tackling this capacity gap by employing consultants, mostly from abroad.

The use of highly paid, "independent" foreign consultants, who are paid in foreign currency and at internationally competitive rates to execute specific adjustment-related tasks, has not only meant that the issue of local-staff pay levels is effectively sidestepped but also bred resentment that has deepened demoralization and, occasionally, inspired acts of sabotage against the consultants and the adjustment process itself. In this context, it is easy to understand why foreign experts are more numerous in crisis-ridden Africa than they were at the dawn of independence in the 1960s.

The nature of success

Although admitting that the SAPs have done little to turn things around in Africa, the BWIs have wanted to highlight a certain number of "success stories," first, to demonstrate that if persistently implemented, the SAPs can lead to recovery and growth and, second, to give African countries models to emulate. The search for success stories has been relentless, at times with tragicomic consequences. It is, therefore, important to look at these experiences in terms of how adequate, replicable, and sustainable they are as strategies for economic development.

The great challenge for those who believe in the "Washington consensus" is to demonstrate that their strategies can achieve the rates of growth enjoyed in the dirigiste era of import substitution and that these rates of growth would be more sustainable than those of the 1960s and 1970s.

Adequacy

An immediate consideration is the degree of success as measured by economic growth. According to the World Bank, the GDP per capita growth of countries that had fair or adequate macroeconomic policies during 1987–91 was 0.4%. At such a growth rate, it would take more than 100 years to double the per capita income of the success stories. Undaunted, the World Bank (1994, p. 6) noted that this was "low but at least positive."

This low but at least positive growth is repeated sectorally. In the case of agriculture, the mean annual growth rate in the strongly adjusting countries actually declined from 3.7% in 1981–86 to 2.0% in 1987–91. Manufacturing achieved a mean annual growth rate of 4.3%, less than that of countries with small improvements. In a continent where negative growth rates have been widespread, such low but positive rates may indeed be something worth being proud of. However, given the performance of Africa in the past, the needs of the continent, and the progress made elsewhere, these low but positive rates are ridiculously low. Their acceptance (and peddling) as "success" can only be understood in terms of the dire straits in which African countries find themselves and a lowering of expectations induced by the bouts of pessimism afflicting the domestic policymakers and the donor community.

The reason for the World Bank's choice of such low performance criteria has been a source of speculation. For example, Helleiner (1994, p. 5) observed that

> the World Bank has consistently understated Africa's medium-term requirements so as to generate aid targets that the major industrialized countries would consider within the range they consider to be politically possible.

According to Lancaster (1991), World Bank staff confirm privately that "realism" about what level of concessional aid is expected to be available plays a role in their calculation of financing gaps and growth targets.

Replicability

Whether the experiences are replicable depends on several things. One of these is, of course, the comparability of initial conditions. Rates of recovery from the depths to which such countries as Ghana, Mozambique, and Uganda had sunk should be understood as perhaps not very surprising. In addition, key adjusting countries received funds to improve their dilapidated infrastructure, and this, rather than adjustment, may have been responsible for the improvements in marketed produce. The levels of funding that some of the star performers received would, under normal circumstances, have led to some of the recovery witnessed in these devastated countries. However, it is doubtful that such levels of funding would be available for many more such experiments in Africa.

Sustainability

A striking feature of the adjustment experience has been the one-off character of the success in moving certain macroeconomic or sectoral indicators in the right direction. This phenomenon shows up in the high turnover of countries listed as success stories. Usually, their appearance on the list is brief, and no sooner are they hailed as strong adjusters than they are relegated to the realm of nonadjusters. This high turnover is often attributed to the high incidence of relapse. This may be true in some cases. However, this might also confirm the critics' point that the policies have largely addressed stabilization and static efficiency issues and have yet to establish mechanisms to ensure structural change and economic growth. The inability of the SAPs to address the structural constraints of these economies might explain why countries enter and drop out of the success-story list at random.

During much of the 1990s, Ghana has been touted as the star performer under adjustment, having the best policy stance and also reaping the bounties of high growth (World Bank 1994). It was rated in this way on the basis of the difference between the average annual growth rates of GDP for the 1980–85 and 1986–92 periods. In recent times, Ghana seems to have disappeared from the list of success stories. Indeed, a recent study of growth in SSA by IMF staff (IMF 1997), using GNP per capita growth rates, classified Ghana among the countries with "weak growth," and 15 other

African countries (including those with serious deterioration in policies according to World Bank criteria) outperformed Ghana. A careful trend analysis of "recovery" in Ghana would reveal that a lot of it consisted of temporary improvements in capacity use. Ghana had huge inflows of donor money to reward progress with adjustment. With the relaxation of balance-of-payments constraints, something in the nature of improved capacity use was bound to happen. The fact that the economy relapsed after the financial inflows ended emphasizes the fragile nature of some of the successes. Not surprisingly, the World Bank quickly found an escape clause to explain Ghana's downturn — "governance problems" (which has become the new slogan in the mid-1990s).

Uganda now bears the flag, joined apparently by Tanzania and some of the franc-zone countries after the CFA franc was devalued. Real GDP grew by an annual average rate of 6.4% between 1991 and 1995, and anecdotal evidence suggests positive effects in terms of employment and performance of the manufacturing sector. Despite the increase in the ratio of tax revenue to GDP from 7% to 12% between 1991 and 1995, Uganda's liberalization may encounter fiscal-incompatibility problems in the near future. In the same way, Uganda's heavy reliance on massive external financing to maintain the payments compatibility of its trade-liberalization process should ring alarm bells. According to the executive director of the Economic Policy Research Centre in Uganda (Opio 1996, p. 12),

> Changes in the flow of external finance are perhaps the most critical in the workings of structural reforms in Uganda. Both official and private transfers net of debt repayments and changes in international terms of trade have played a vital role in the implementation of SAP in Uganda. Given persistent negative terms of trade, aid inflows in Uganda have become a substitute to export earnings, and yet insufficient to off-set the combined negative effects of changes in the terms of trade and debt service. Uganda has continued to enjoy concessional aid, since the introduction of SAP, which must have accounted for much of her success in the implementation of structural reforms.

One obvious source of the nonsustainability of such success is that thus far it has failed to increase domestic savings to levels that would allow the economy to maintain the high growth rate without a massive injection of foreign capital. The failure to ensure long-term sustainability through higher levels of investment and savings is a natural outcome of the emphasis on stabilization "fundamentals."

Extent of reform and degree of compliance

We have discussed the African experience on the assumption that a number of countries have experimented with structural adjustment. Some of these countries have been strong adjusters for a considerable length of time. However, a new line of argument is that African countries have, in fact, hardly begun to adjust. Because it is a line that we are likely to hear more of, a word or two on this may be appropriate in closing this chapter.

No matter what one thinks about the SAPs, it is clear that African economies have been subject to dramatic reforms in the last decade or so. The state's presence in the economy has been rolled back, markets have been given much greater space, and African economies are much more open to private capital than ever before. Are these reforms enough? The World Bank has itself vacillated between euphoria over the extent of economic reform and anger at slippage or lack of commitment to reform. In *Adjustment in Africa*, the World Bank (1994) blamed poor performance on poor implementation of the SAPs, which were assumed to be the right prescription. Had the extent of slippage been much less and had African governments not tended to fall back on their retrograde interventionist or profligate ways, adjustment would have worked.

The dominant current explanation for the failure of reform has three strands. One involves the explanations for the significant "Africa dummy" in econometric comparisons of growth performance. The second states that not enough time has elapsed to allow for the programs to be implemented. The third (often linked to the first) is that there has been too much slippage.

The exceptionally poor performance of African economies under the SAPs has raised questions about the specificities of the African case. Answering these questions has become a kind of cottage industry. The new endogenous-growth theory has provided a powerful tool for explicating the channels through which policy and nonpolicy variables affect growth. In the last several years, the need to explain the observed and unaccountably persisting African economic crisis has spawned a growing number of empirical studies using cross-country growth and investment regressions. Such a methodology is evidently of the ad hoc, add-and-drop kind: researchers repeatedly experimented, by trial and error, with alternative definitions and variables until the expected results were obtained. With a methodology that is sensitive to the choice and definition of variables, as well as to country and time coverage, virtually every analyst found enough variables to significantly explain Africa's poor performance. Initially, much of this literature emanated from the World Bank staff and served mainly to validate the Bank's view that domestic policies were to blame for the crisis. External factors were found either to be insignificant or to matter only in the short run.

Over time, however, the debate has broadened, and a wider array of explanatory variables has been found (see Collier and Gunning [1997] for a survey of some of the empirical literature). Variables featured in many of these regressions include trade restrictions; lack of openness to trade; lack of financial depth; deficient public service and infrastructural provision; lack of social capital; high macroeconomic volatility and uncertainty; terms-of-trade shocks; drought; offsetting effects of aid; and external-debt burden. Social and political characteristics of Africa are receiving growing attention — these are proxied by the strength of civil society; corruption; bureaucratic red-tapeism; enforceability of contracts; civil war; ethnolinguistic fractionalization; governance; and so forth. Surprisingly, researchers cannot account for the very high residual that remains, even after controlling for all these variables. The implication, of course, is a disquieting pointer that even if African countries get all the prescribed policy fundamentals and enabling environment right, high growth performance would not be guaranteed. Increasingly, attention is focusing on things peculiar to Africa, and several new explanations point to the atypically high natural-resource endowments and high levels of ethnic fractionalization. Basically, what the use of this last set of variables seems to be saying is that Africa is the way it is because of its inherent characteristics, and policy and external environment have little to do with it.

All the variables, taken as a group, still fail to explain much of Africa's slow growth. As Collier and Gunning (1997, p. 15) argued, "no regression based on the variables discussed above has yet convincingly eliminated the significance of the African dummy variable: Africa has grown unaccountably slowly." Referring to the significance of certain variables in an investment regression, Collier and Gunning (1997, pp. 16–17) also noted that

> On the whole, the econometric evidence thus vindicates Bank–IMF liberalisation programmes, the centrepiece of which has been trade and exchange rate liberalisation and greater fiscal stability. However, this gives rise to a new puzzle. Despite a decade of Bank–IMF liberalisation programmes, as we have seen, African performance has remained poor.

The authors argued that the three main explanations for the disappointing performance despite the SAPs were "low implementation, insufficient time for observable effects, and the effects of risk" (Collier and Gunning 1997, p. 18).

Although there is a grain of truth in these explanations, many analysts would doubt that these factors explain a significant part of the enduring crisis. Furthermore, implementation effort and risk are both endogenous variables, and each is tied to the behaviour of a country's government. This suggests the need for a careful understanding of the constraints that policymakers face in designing and implementing policies. On the other hand, the riskiness of the African investment climate is probably a deterrent to investment, but it is unlikely to be the critical factor. For example, in the 1970–80 and 1991–94 periods, Nigeria was among the 10 developing countries receiving the largest amounts of FDI (and certainly the country receiving the largest amount of such investment in the whole of Africa). During 1991–96, Nigeria and Angola were the most and second most attractive countries for flows of FDI in Africa. It would be simplistic to argue that this was because Nigeria and Angola were countries with the least risk for investors or, for that matter, that the current star performers in Africa have the most risk-free investment environments. Although objective conditions for calculating country risk exist, for much of Africa the problem might be more one of perception than one of reality. Our hypothesis is that even if we control for risk and implementation effort, a large chunk of the African growth residual would still remain unexplained.

In both cases, it is now argued that the Bretton Woods institutions have actually failed to effectively impose their conditionality. The debate on conditionality and slippage is increasingly conducted within the principal–agent framework (Killick 1996; Mosley 1996). The donors are the principals, who are seeking adjustment and sound economic policy, and the African governments are the agents, who are only interested in the money. The question then is how the agent can be monitored and induced to behave in a manner that minimizes moral hazard, slippage, and so forth. Whatever the merits of this approach, it does point to the extent that the discourse on policy-making has displaced national governments from the central position and reduced them to agents performing activities in which they have no intrinsic interest. A number of problems arise with most of these arguments.

First, the poor performance of a number of strong adjusters and the good performance of some of the poor adjusters within obviously very small samples raise questions about the real importance of implementing the SAPs. Indeed, the evidence is that the progress may be as much due to aspects of the SAPs implemented as it is to aspects not implemented. Second, the objective of adjustment is increasingly a moving target. Even in evaluating past reforms, analysts can reach no agreement about when reform really started. Different World Bank reports have, over the years, used different periods. The 1994 reports took 1987 as the year when adjustment started. In their turn, Collier and Gunning (1997) argued that reform had been going on for no more than only a couple of years in most countries. In addition, it is never clearly stated how much reform is required to get what level of performance and over what period. Indeed, the argument for reform as stated is essentially unfalsifiable. That is to say, if a country introduced reforms one year and enjoyed growth the next year, then the growth is attributed to the reform, but if no growth occurred, it is argued that 1 year was not enough, and if negative growth occurs, then appeal is made to exogenous factors such as terms of trade and, increasingly, the Procrustean concepts of governance and risk. Matters are compounded by the high turnover of good performers. Few of them stay on the list for more than 3 years before they are inexplicably dropped. For example, the major task of the two-volume World Bank (1994) report was to demonstrate that adjustment works. Many countries were classified as having had large improvements in policies (with Ghana as the star adjuster), and the report tried to rigorously show that those countries outperformed their counterparts that had experienced deterioration in policies.

According to the World Bank (1994) report, therefore, several countries had had effective implementation, at least up to 1994. Suddenly, however, Ghana and many of the countries identified in that report as strong adjusters dropped out of the performance list, and new ones — Côte d'Ivoire, Ethiopia, Uganda, and so forth — came in. To argue, as Collier and Gunning (1997) do, that the relevant time frame for evaluating adjustment should be the 1990s simply because that's when these current stars started adjustment amplifies the presence of tautology in the debate. The authors need to show either that the World Bank's previous studies were wrong about the adjustment efforts in Africa or that what most African countries have implemented since the early 1980s was not adjustment. Another essential point to emphasize is that although we celebrate the current stars, we must not lose sight of the fact that we have always had star performers at any point in time. Why do countries enter and drop out of the good-performance list? Are such star performances temporary spurts generated by improvements in external conditions — ostensibly greater aid inflows, good weather, and preferable terms of trade — or are they wholly attributable to implementation? And can the current stars sustain the successes?

Perhaps it is more significant that in much of this debate, it is never considered whether the SAPs are a fatally flawed remedy for the deep structural problems that African research institutions have been stressing for many years. No attempts are made to rethink the model itself in the light of both this poor performance and the lessons of the Asian miracle. Instead, one sees a furtive search for instruments for imposing this particular model of adjustment on Africans by eliciting or organizing domestic social forces favourable to it, or by improving the administrative and governance capacity of the state, or by finding external agents of restraint.

Chapter 4

Widening the Road Ahead

Every reasonable analysis of the adjustment process in Africa so far returns the same verdict: it has not succeeded in laying the foundations for sustainable growth and development. The contraction, treated as an inevitable but necessary phase, has placed African economies on a low growth path, and rates of growth hardly higher than population growth are heralded as success. If this course is taken as sacrosanct, such rates of growth can only widen the gap between Africa and other countries and, even more seriously, are unlikely to make a dent in the poverty that haunts much of Africa. A few facts about African economies in the late 1990s, after years of adjustment, are worth reviewing.

Macroeconomic stability has improved modestly, but many analysts doubt that it will be sustainable, given that in most economies in which it has occurred, volatile external finance has been largely responsible for the improvement. Moreover, stability has been achieved mostly at the expense of domestic investment, even in basic infrastructure (physical infrastructure and human-capital formation) that has been recognized as being central to sustainable growth and development. As Nissanke (1997, p. 6) argued,

> The present narrow base for raising fiscal and export revenues means also a continuous implementation of short-term stabilisation policies on a perpetual basis, leaving the economies constantly exposed to large external shocks, as primary commodity prices in the world market exhibit not only declining long-term trends but also excessively volatile fluctuations which are detrimental to growth and development. Sub-Saharan African countries have to undertake continuous adjustments to their deteriorating and highly unstable position in current account balance. The scale of adjustment required has often far exceeded the capacity of these economies to absorb and manage volatilities associated with high uncertainty and aggregate systemic risks.

Modest recovery in output (essentially improved capacity use in most cases) has been uneven and fragile, with economies entering and dropping out of the good-or-excellent performance list. That is why, despite the fragile but encouraging aggregate performance of African economies in 1996, it must be cautioned that such a recovery might not be sustainable in view of the structural weaknesses and heavy debt burden.

The external debt of SSA has more than doubled over the adjustment period, without any increase in economic growth to sustain its servicing in the future. Africa's infrastructural base and human-capital formation, which were deemed to be fragile at the beginning of adjustment, have deteriorated even further. Africa's capacity to manage the crisis has been further eroded through massive brain drain and demoralization of the civil service, caused by sharply declining real wages, massive retrenchment, and the incessant vilification of civil servants as corrupt members of corrupt institutions.

Despite modest recovery in some countries, poverty has intensified, and human-development indicators — life expectancy, infant mortality, and school enrolment — have worsened. The export basket remains undiversified, and although a recovery of about 3.2% in exports has been achieved, imports have grown by an average of 6.4% (due mainly to import liberalization). Given the external-debt burden, the balance-of-payments feasibility of these economies remains in serious doubt. Since the start of the adjustment programs the fragile industrial base has shrunk even further (deindustrialization) in many countries.

The African states, already weak before the adjustment programs were initiated, have become even weaker, and the requisite institutions for development are either very weak or nonexistent in some countries.

After nearly two decades of debates, costly experimentation with variants of the SAPs, and sustained challenges posed by UNECA's African Alternative Framework to Structural Adjustment Programs, the recent writings and pronouncements of most Africans demonstrate a convergence toward some African perspective on the way forward. It is increasingly asserted that Africans need to reclaim the driver's seat in articulating the solution for their economic-development problems. The emerging consensus derives from the facts, summarized above, as well as from lessons learned about the kinds of policies that are required, the ones that can work, and the issues that should be addressed. This is a perspective informed by the lessons derivable from the experiences of more successful economies, especially in Asia, and by a fuller appreciation of the constraints and opportunities offered by the new and continuously evolving international environment. This is a perspective informed by the recognition that far-reaching global changes have occurred and that Africa needs to redefine its position in a global, highly competitive market. This is a perspective informed by the belief that Africa can and should be allowed to compete, with a full appreciation of the constraints imposed by increasing globalization and with an understanding of demands of time and the imperatives of sound policies to overcome underdevelopment in the shortest possible time. A "sound but developmentalist" policy framework is underscored because, given the dire economic malaise of the subregion, the lost time, and the mistakes of the past, the need to place African economies on a development path is extremely urgent.

In this chapter, we summarize the key strands of such a sound but developmentalist policy perspective, which, among other things, includes stabilization cum efficiency-enhancing, market-compatible policies, combined with key developmentalist policy fundamentals to enhance resource mobilization, investment, and equity.

Broadening the fundamentals

"Getting the fundamentals" right is now a commonly asserted prerequisite for economic growth. No one would disagree. What is debatable is the nature of those fundamentals and of the edifice they are supposed to support. Our view is that a perspective on policy fundamentals must simultaneously address the following issues: equity, economic growth, economic stability, and political legitimacy. The weight attached to each of these will depend on each country's political and economic conditions. Each model of adjustment suggests what the fundamentals are. We contend that the SAP is a kind of adjustment that has increasingly considered stabilization issues as being the fundamentals and has failed to see the importance of a much broader list.

Beyond stabilization fundamentals

In times of economic turbulence and scarce resources, concern with stabilization tends to attain great prominence on the policy agenda, and monetary and financial fundamentals have tended to be confined to issues of stability and efficiency in the use of given resources. The crisis of the last two decades has underscored the importance of macroeconomic stability to the extent that in some circles, it is widely considered a necessary condition for restoring growth. Countries are now routinely required to enter into agreement with the IMF before getting access to other sources of funding.

Without doubt, macroeconomic stability is of importance to both the economic and the political well-being of a country. No sustainable growth can be seriously expected in a context of hyperinflation and unsustainable balance-of-payments disequilibrium. Thus, any new policy must address issues of stability and must seek to get the financial fundamentals in place, not necessarily sequentially but at least simultaneously with the other fundamentals we discuss later. African policymakers not only need to take issues of stabilization seriously — cutting wasteful spending where necessary (for example, military spending, subsidies to nonperforming public enterprises, and redundant public-works schemes) — but also need to improve the capacity and efficiency of incentives that are compatible with revenue generation.

We noted how preoccupation with development issues of the 1960s and 1970s and the consequent little regard for macroeconomic stabilization were partly responsible for the debt and balance-of-payments crisis of the 1980s. In reaction to this, there has been a rush to stabilization policies without regard for the negative consequences of these policies on investment, employment, and the process of technological learning.

Indeed, the financial system gives deteriorating support to the production system and tends to give primacy to the exigencies of financial stabilization, even when these undermine economic production and social cohesion. Although financial stabilization perhaps addresses issues of static allocative efficiency and perhaps is appropriate for this narrow perception of fundamentals, stabilization policies fail to explicitly incorporate measures to address developmental fundamentals and in themselves fail to guarantee the resumption of growth. The implication is that there is a distinct danger they will produce a "poor but stable and efficient" Africa or, in the words of Helleiner (1994),

> "Getting prices right" and keeping them stable and reasonably "right" is an important part, but of course, only a part, of long-run development policy. Without human capital and accumulation, investment, access to technology, etc., "correct" prices will only increase the efficiency with which one stagnates.

To make matters worse, even domestic decision-makers, especially ministries of finance, have latched onto this exclusive obsession with stabilization. Thus, Lancaster (1991) reported that

> The priority placed on balance of payments stabilisation, debt servicing, and closing of a balance of payments financing gap (rather than an import financing gap associated with target rates of growth) is often echoed in developing country governments where ministries of finance rather than development agencies typically take the lead in shaping their governments' positions on stabilisation and debt-rescheduling agreements, which often precede or are taken independently of government positions on structural adjustment programs and development financing.

After the promise of "accelerated development" of 1981 (World Bank 1981) and the promise of "sustainable development" in 1989 (World Bank 1989b) and the more recent *Adjustment in Africa* (World Bank 1994), "development" disappeared from the adjustment discourse to such an extent that the success indicators were confined to the movement of policy instruments, rather than the real economy. A country was doing well if it entered into an agreement with BWIs or if it reduced its deficits.

In the World Bank's (1989b) *Sub-Saharan Africa: From Crisis to Sustainable Growth*, the Bank attempted to assert the developmental thrust of adjustment. The 1989 report recognized the importance of structural and institutional factors in explaining economic performance in Africa. It correctly pointed out that

> It is not sufficient for African governments merely to consolidate the progress made in their adjustment programs. They need to go beyond the issues of public finance, monetary policy, prices and markets to address fundamental questions relating to human capacities, institutions, governance, the environment, population growth and distribution, and technology.

The report suggested that human resources, technology, regional cooperation, self-reliance, and respect for African values provide the main focus of a proposed strategy. This strategy stressed the need to establish an enabling environment for infrastructure services and incentives to foster efficient production and private initiative and enhance the capacities of people and institutions — a growth strategy must be both sustainable and equitable.

This was a significant broadening of perspective for the World Bank and was in some ways a move closer to the position that UNECA had been promoting for many years. To be sure, the notion of governance was excessively technocratic and narrow. However, it led to a much less jaundiced view of the role of the state in the economy and placed issues of governance at the core of the policy dialogue. This shift was, however, short-lived and was de-emphasized in *Adjustment in Africa* (World Bank 1994). The report used indices of policy stance that said nothing about other fundamentals. The composite index was made up of

- Fiscal policy, identified by the size of the deficit;
- Monetary stance, based on seigniorage, inflation, and the real interest rate; and
- Exchange-rate policy stance.

Nothing was said about proactive policies required by a dynamic industrial policy, a transformative agrarian process of Green Revolution dimensions, and the accumulation of both physical and human capital at a forced, more rapid pace. One should recall that many development-inducing policies are of a micro- or mesolevel nature. The primacy given to stabilization fundamentals led to a confusion between microeconomic policies and macroeconomic ones, with microlevel policies presumed "guilty by association" with the failed macroeconomic ones (Rodrik 1995).

Under the current reforms, the emphasis on getting the monetary and financial accounts and the fundamentals right has almost become an end in itself because it has been assumed that most other microeconomic or sectoral issues would be automatically resolved by such reforms. The result has been that interventionist microeconomic policies that had worked in the high-performing East Asian economies (HPEAs) were rejected wholesale, leaving the state with virtually nothing to do in the development process. Experiences so far in most parts of the world, including Europe, point to the need to take explicit steps to get other fundamentals right. For example, the quest for the European common currency has imposed an emphasis on monetary and fiscal fundamentals, with complete disregard for the "real" side of the economy. Many countries are realizing that the adjustment costs are simply too enormous, and it is not surprising that many newly elected governments in Britain, France, etc. are arguing that employment and output should be targets for monetary union.

Toward development fundamentals

Griffin (1996) identified three paths of adjustment, each emphasizing a different set of fundamentals.

The first path is adjustment by correction of distorted prices. Correction of prices will lead to changes along the production function such that the composition of outputs will favour commodities in which a country has comparative advantage. Thus, contraction in, for example, manufacturing, will be compensated for by increases in mining or agriculture. This is the model implicit in orthodox prescriptions to remove distortions. The concern here is with allocating a given amount of resources more efficiently, and the movement is along a given production function. A variant of this strategy would involve the removal of a number of bottlenecks to get the economy back to its previous production-function recovery, with no mechanism in place for subsequent growth.

The second path is adjustment by contraction. This strategy involves contraction of unprofitable activities but without accompanying growth in output in the profitable sectors. Resources released from unprofitable sectors may simply not be usable in profitable sectors because of the specificity of both capital and labour. In addition, the investment funds needed for resource reallocation may simply not be available. The factor combinations may be much like those of the first kind of adjustment but at a contracted level. This has been the pattern of adjustment in Africa.

The third path is adjustment through investment. This strategy involves investment in new activities and measures to improve the productivity of some hitherto unproductive activities. It involves a shot on a higher production curve along a path with a more efficient combination of sectors. This, Griffin (1996) suggested, seems to be the path chosen by China and Viet Nam.

The fundamentals defined exclusively by stabilization needs are most likely to produce adjustment by contraction or recovery. To create the conditions of an investment-driven development process, policy must be founded on a much more complex set of fundamentals than the ones suggested above. A critical element of the emerging consensus of views is that macroeconomic stability sensitive to the real side of the economy (both social and material) is an important element of a strategy of economic growth and development. Financial fundamentals must be compatible with, and indeed secondary to, other fundamentals that ensure political stability and economic growth.

A broad spectrum of African analysts (both academic and official) have insisted that development-focused adjustment should simultaneously establish fundamentals relating to the financial, production, and governance systems that constitute a development-policy package. In more recent times, one additional set of fundamentals relates to the environmental sustainability of economic growth. The presumption in all these is the view that economic policies in Africa will be judged by the extent to which they contribute to economic development, which is broadly understood as involving economic growth, structural change, and the elimination of poverty. Our thesis is that policy must simultaneously address a broad range of fundamentals: macroeconomic-stabilization fundamentals; proactive, supply-side (production) fundamentals; and sociopolitical fundamentals. All these are mutually reinforcing.

Production fundamentals

Production fundamentals address the real side of structural variables — productivity, demand for output, firm and household behaviour, institutional relations, innovation process, tangible and intangible investment, export orientation, employment creation, and economic growth. A development-oriented adjustment program will be investment driven. Therefore, policy must include measures to increase investment and improve allocation among sectors and projects. This applies to both public and private investment. The new growth theories stress the importance of increasing labour productivity through learning-by-doing innovation, but they also stress the need to accumulate substantial capital to put innovations into practice and ensure widespread employment.

Under the SAPs, the relative importance of microeconomic signals reflecting trade, industrial, and other policies has declined. In the 1960s, policy reforms were directed to rationalization of microlevel incentives and improved efficiency of investments. These policies lay behind the choice of industries for import substitution and public investment. Such policies have become less pronounced since the 1980s. However, even strategies to develop export markets need to have more than just the financial fundamentals in place. Deliberate microlevel polices are needed to provide signals to private investors.

INDUSTRIALIZATION OF AFRICA

The industrialization of Africa is still high on the agenda, despite the battering it has suffered in recent years. Not only must African countries aim to reverse the process of deindustrialization, but also they must actively seek to catch up to others with unprecedented speed. Experience from the high-performing Asian countries clearly suggests the importance of strategies and interventionist policies for rapid industrialization, in contrast to the didactic messages about market friendliness extracted from the story of the East Asian miracle.

TRADE POLICY FOR INDUSTRIALIZATION

Africa's position in the new global-trade relations will be largely determined by the actions it takes in two important directions:

- It should increase the regional and international competitiveness of its production activities by changing the export structure to include more dynamic, nontraditional products (in terms of their demand prospects and their potential to effect technological change); and
- It should tackle the structural bottlenecks inherent in the entire system of governance and specifically address export promotion and industrial development.

The need to change the export structure will inevitably steer the development agenda back to policy issues relating to export diversification, transformation of production structures, and industrialization.

Perhaps one of the most controversial areas of economic policy under the SAPs was the recommendation of "incentive-neutral" trade policy and the associated perfect-competition and comparative-advantage models that underlie the attendant industrialization strategy. Trade policy under the adjustment programs has entailed a gamut of measures to reduce domestic policy distortions, open the economy to international competition, and, in the process, ensure a more neutral incentive structure that does not discriminate between exportables and importables or between production for the domestic market and production for exports. For industry, this implies the negation of industrial policy. There would be no need for industrial policy if markets worked perfectly; if there were competitive markets with no economies of scale, perfect information, and no risk or uncertainty; and if firms operated with full knowledge of all possible technologies, with equal access to them, and with the ability to use them efficiently without risk, cost, or additional effort. Further, the model does not recognize missing or defective markets and assumes that comparative advantage in industry, as given by resource endowments, will be realized. Thus, because previous government interventions, along with wasteful, inefficient trade restrictions and import-substitution strategies for industrialization, are to blame for poor performance, the remedy lies in immediate and sweeping liberalization of trade as the most efficient way to reform.

This single-minded focus on getting the prices right as the panacea for the trade and industrial problems of African economies has elicited severe criticisms from several scholars. In the first instance, many scholars question any relationship between trade and growth and, in particular, a causality running from trade to growth (Taylor 1983; Bradford 1994; Felix 1994; Helleiner 1994; Young 1994; Singh 1995). Regarding industrial policies, many other analysts and the new trade theorists strongly challenge the neoclassical assumptions underlying industrialization and trade strategies for Africa (Lall and Stewart 1996; Soludo 1997, 1998; Wangwe and Semboja 1998).

After years of debate and accumulation of empirical evidence, a consensus is emerging. First, it is generally agreed that Africans would greatly benefit from trade in a variety of ways, not the least of which would be improvement in the balance of payments and increased foreign-exchange earnings from exports, which could be used to buy imports. Even the more sceptical scholars are beginning to appreciate that greater trade is growth inducing, especially when a country has increased the share of manufactures in its exports. The experiences of the East Asian economies corroborate this. Second, there seems to be a broader convergence of views on the claim that a reform of the previous trade regime (some trade liberalization) has wide-ranging benefits, but key controversies pertain to the nature, coverage, magnitude, timing, and sequencing of such a liberalization scheme. Third, African and development scholars generally agree that diversifying the production structures — shifting the focus from dependence on primary commodities toward a competitive manufacturing sector — is a desideratum for sustainable growth and development. In terms of policy, the emerging perspective is one that broadly acknowledges the need for a rethinking of past policies, that admits the central roles of a competitive exchange-rate regime, market forces, and private initiative, but that argues that in late-coming industrializers such as the SSA countries, these forces need to be managed with appropriate state-interventionist policies to resolve pervasive market failures.

A major difference between the trade regimes of the more successful East Asian economies and those of Africa and Latin America during the 1960s and 1970s is that the former combined import substitution with export promotion, whereas the latter concentrated almost exclusively on import substitution. An important lesson is that the two aspects of trade strategy (import and export policies) can have different implications that should be carefully considered in any policy reform. The Asian experience demonstrates that an effective export-promotion strategy could be accompanied by a restrictive import policy. This experience shows an astoundingly successful use of trade policy, not only for balance-of-payments purposes but, more so, for the promotion of effective industrialization through graduated infant-industry protection. In the light of this Asian experience and the recent experiences of several SSA countries, any trade strategy must carefully address both the import and the export sides of trade policy, with a view to making them consistent with the objectives of achieving rapid industrialization and sustainable balance-of-payments status.

The import side presents the most controversial aspect of trade policy. The typical SAP recommendation is a target of 10% uniform tariff rates for all imports of manufactures to be achieved over the medium term (typically about 3 years); the only reason for phasing the tariff reduction should be for revenue purposes. The SAPs apparently see no reason to retain protection for infant industries, to graduate the liberalization process according to the speed of relearning and the development of the relevant factor markets, or to discriminate between activities according to their different technological and restructuring needs. There is neither theoretical nor empirical support for this approach. Indeed, a recent World Bank (1996) survey of manufacturing in Africa argued that "regarding trade policy, there is no a priori reason why Africa should not benefit from some form of infant industry protection to promote learning in domestic firms, as has been evident in cases of most successful developers in this century."

Evidently, in much of SSA, the traditional instruments of trade policy, such as import tariffs and quantitative import restrictions, are often used to serve multiple objectives because of the peculiar characteristics of these economies, which limit the availability and effectiveness of other instruments. For example, relative to other regions, Africa has the narrowest sources of government revenue and thus the highest dependence on trade taxes for revenue. An abrupt and unplanned liberalization, without any compensating source of revenue, is likely to be inconsistent with the requirements to maintain fiscal discipline. It is, therefore, of little surprise that most of the liberalization attempts have encountered severe budgetary problems.

Given the already precarious balance-of-payments situation of most African countries, a deep, generalized, and sudden import liberalization can induce an abnormally high demand for imports, thereby worsening the current account. In an SAP framework requiring macroeconomic stability (ostensibly through deficit reduction) and current-account survival, simultaneous implementation of deep import liberalization conflicts with these objectives, as recent experiences demonstrate. Furthermore, the timely and effective diversification of the production and export sector into manufacturing cannot be contemplated without some protection for the infant industries, such as a differential tariff structure and even export incentives. The relative weights attached by policymakers to these concerns would probably determine the future direction, scope, and speed of import liberalization in SSA. In general, the emerging perspective seems to favour a more graduated liberalization program. A recent ILO report (ILO 1996, p. 157) summed up the perspective by arguing that

> A radical, across-the-board trade liberalisation as part of a "big bang" strategy is likely to lead to unnecessarily high social costs. As mentioned earlier, imports would increase rapidly while exports can only increase more gradually. This problem would be compounded where there is little real effective devaluation of the exchange rate. As a result, job losses would greatly exceed job creation and there would, at the same time, be strong pressure on the balance of payments. There is thus a case for a more gradual and selective approach to trade liberalisation.

Under this graduated approach to liberalization, the often recommended sequence is to gradually reduce and remove the import quotas and licences, replace them with tariffs, and then lower and simplify the tariffs. Tariffication (replacement of quantitative restrictions with tariffs) is preferred because it is more transparent, and predictable than nontariff restrictions and hence less susceptible to corruptive manipulation. Furthermore, tariffs generate government revenue. It is reasonable to say that the speed of the lowering and rationalization of tariffs should depend on each country's initial conditions and the response of its export sector. Policymakers and implementers should, however, be careful that the gradual liberalization does not run the risk of being captured or frustrated by some vested interest groups. The tariff structure should be fairly simple, with a limited number of tariff rates, to ensure greater transparency.

The export side of the trade policy and, in particular, the need to promote aggressive export orientation have received great attention for self-evident reasons. Beyond the economies of scale and efficiency gains from such orientation, more compelling reasons for Africa to promote exports pertain to balance-of-payments considerations and the need to earn foreign exchange to import production inputs. The typical World Bank recommendation for export promotion is to ensure a neutral trade regime that treats imports and exports similarly. In particular, the World Bank (1994, p. 192) advised that in promoting exports, "governments should not try to pick **winners**. ... Governments can best help entrepreneurs discover and develop competitive exports by getting out of the way." Such a conclusion either seems to be based on the presumption that African governments are inherently incapable of carrying out the simplest of choices or stems from an appeal to arguments about the effectiveness of industrial policy that may make sense in countries at a more advanced stage of economic development. In either case, it is wrong.

First, no case has been made to demonstrate why African policymakers cannot learn from others, and, second, the World Bank develops the process of picking winners into an arcane art form that is beyond African capacities. Yet, as a report of the United Nations Conference on Trade and Development (UNCTAD 1996, p. 22) noted,

> Unlike developed countries, developing countries are not initially operating at the technological frontier of international best practice. Consequently promoting industrial development does not involve their picking winners in an uncertain technological race based on innovation, but lifting the propensity to invest and promoting movements along existing learning curves, including how to acquire mastery over readily available technologies and how to compete in mature-product markets with already established firms.

We noted that a central orthodox recommendation for industrial policy is to establish a neutral trade regime favouring neither imports nor exports. The emphasis in neoclassical theory on a neutral trade regime derives from the argument that a protective import regime — through tariffs and nontariff barriers — is inconsistent with export orientation (antiexport bias). The argument is that import restrictions constitute a tax on exports. By making import substitutes relatively more profitable, they increase the costs and reduce the availability of imported inputs used in the production of exports, thereby forcing exporters to use relatively expensive and low-quality locally produced inputs. Import restrictions, through the sub-stitution effects, also lead to an appreciation of the real exchange rate, which hurts exports. These consequences need not materialize. First, the alleged appre-ciation of the real exchange rate resulting from import restrictions is empirically questionable. Second, the antiexport bias can be eliminated by implementing a differentiated tariff structure that discriminates in favour of imported production inputs. For example, schemes that grant exporters and their suppliers unrestricted access to imported and locally produced inputs at internationally competitive prices can be implemented. Export-processing zones, duty-drawback or duty-exemption schemes, and bonded warehousing arrangements are some of the ways to eliminate the antiexport bias without maintaining the overall import tariff rates at floor levels. In other words, export promotion and import substitution are not necessarily inconsistent aspects of a trade policy.

Another important question that arises is whether there should be a sequencing process between import liberalization and export promotion. This question is of great importance in SSA, given the recent experiences with import liberalization and the associated deindustrialization and heightened balance-of-payments crisis. In foreign-exchange-constrained economies, exports provide the critical means for purchasing increased imports made available through trade liberalization. Thus, a good export performance (to earn foreign exchange) is critical to sustaining import liberalization. In the light of this, some scholars argue that in countries with clearly defined development strategies and adequate capacity to implement them, appropriate export-promotion measures can be used to ensure out-ward orientation before a full-scale import liberalization is implemented.

A salient point that should be emphasized here is that adequate preparations should be made — in terms of relevant supply-side measures and institutional arrangements — to elicit the desired export supply responses before deep liberalization schemes are implemented. The experi-ences of Argentina, Brazil, Zimbabwe, and (to some extent) Mauritius bear this out. In Mauritius and Zimbabwe, trade liberalization was managed more selectively in a context in which the export sector was already quite diversified and firms had attained a reasonable degree of competitiveness. Firms were given adequate time to make adjustments. In the specific case of Zimbabwe, import liberalization started with imported inputs through a form of generalized import-licencing scheme. Users of this preferential scheme were made aware that the next phase of import liberalization would allow the import of goods that would compete with their outputs. This message, therefore, induced many firms to invest in technological improvements of various kinds in anticipation of a more competitive environment. In contrast, the case of Zambia provides an example of how not to liberalize. Industrial performance deteriorated after liberalization. This cannot be attributed only to the inefficiency of the firms; the explanation must also include the inefficiency in the firms' operating environment (for example, distortions in financial markets, high import protection for input providers, and high energy costs). These factors were not dealt with before or in conjunction with the introduction of the liberalization measures.

Furthermore, in deciding whether to pursue a big bang approach to liberalization or a gradualist approach, one should bear in mind the implications for accumulated human capital in particular industries. Given that a certain amount of capability development has already taken place in the industrial sector, one should endeavour to conserve this valuable resource, rather than allowing it to dissipate through shock therapy that only leads to massive deindustrialization. Technological capabilities reside in groups of skilled and experienced persons, rather than in individuals. The destruction of enterprises therefore means that the stock of accumulated knowledge is effectively destroyed, even if the individuals concerned stay in the country. This important feature of industrialization is ignored by the SAPs, but it has been vital to the policy approach of the East Asian newly industrialized economies.

The foregoing discussion of the nature and sequence of trade liberalization obviously has enormous implications for the diversification and competitiveness of the industrial sector. In practice, however, the difference between trade and industrial policies has become blurred because they are complementary. The gradual trade-liberalization model and, more so, the suggestion that adequate supply-side, export-promotion infrastructure be put in place before or in conjunction with liberalization are both consistent with the emerging perspective on sound industrialization strategy. In addition to recognizing the failures of past ISI strategies, this perspective acknowledges two other major sources of the failures of African industrialization:

- Pervasive external shocks, especially the worsening terms of trade and external-debt burden that drain scarce foreign exchange and starve African industry of essential imported inputs, have caused industry to stagnate; and

- The weak industrial capabilities and deficient institutions in Africa, as structuralist economists point out, have frustrated industrialists' attempts to become efficient in modern industrial activity.

These constraints have led several scholars to argue that the objective of getting the prices right might be just one of the fundamentals but by no means the dominant one in determining industrial efficiency and competitiveness. As Lall and Stewart (1996, pp. 187–188) have shown,

> Recent research on technological learning in developing countries suggests that industrialization is far more complex and varied than the neo-classical model assumes. Becoming efficient in industry can be a slow, risky, costly, and prolonged process, beset by a range of market failures that call for interventions in both factor and product markets — for example, missing information markets, asymmetric information, externalities, technical linkages, unpredictable learning sequences, deficient capital markets, and absence of supporting institutions and skills.

Another study (UNCTAD 1996, p. 16) corroborated the above assertion by arguing that

> It is not generally possible to rely on market forces alone to move economies through these various stages of industrialisation and export orientation, on account of a number of market failures related to externalities, problems of co-ordination, imperfect and asymmetric information, economies of scale, missing markets and imperfect competition. Since these factors impose themselves on the pace and direction of the industrialisation process, the question of how best to manage this process gains in importance.

On the basis of these observations, there seems to be an emerging consensus among some analysts about the potential policy implications, which greatly modify the neoclassical single-minded focus on prices. A poor African country attempting to venture into a new industry finds that it must compete with already established firms in developed countries with vastly superior technology (and also superior managerial skills, financial abilities, and even intangible assets such as brand-name loyalty). In the presence of competition, "it is very difficult for the firms from a poor country to survive in their own domestic market, not to speak of breaking into export markets, if free trade prevails" (Chang 1996, p. 11). The implication is that some protection or subsidization of the infant industry would be required initially before exposing it to international competition. In essence, without protection for several industrial activities with strong learning and scale economies, such activities might never even develop at all, and deindustrialization might occur if existing firms are exposed to full, and sudden, international competition.

However, adherents of this view also warn against the kind of previous protection that prevented infant industries from maturing. It is recognized that such protection, among other things, has some social-welfare costs. However, as Chang (1996, p. 6) pointed out,

> The loss in current social welfare through infant industry protection is a necessary price that has to be paid for industrial development in a poor country in the long run, but the country should try to keep such price low by avoiding infant industry promotions of excessive magnitude and duration. Of course, the important question then is what exactly is "excessive," but the experience of the East Asian countries suggests that the magnitude and the duration of feasible infant industry protection are much greater than what is usually accepted by mainstream economists.

Dell (1982, p. 602) provided further justification for this policy stance by arguing that

> There is not a single industrial country that did not employ vigorous protection at some stage in its history. Among the much applauded newly industrialising countries ... the most important have highly regulated economies. Even so highly industrialised a country as Japan, the miracle economy of the century, continues to this day to protect its industrial development in a variety of ways. While Japan is under great pressure to dismantle this protection, the important lesson of Japan for the developing countries and for the Fund is that properly managed protection, so far from being an obstacle to growth, is an indispensable instrument in promoting growth.

Furthermore, Dell (1982, p. 603) articulated the common argument of those opposed to government interventions but dismissed such objections:

> Where there is a case against regulation, it depends not on any inherent superiority of market forces, but on the much simpler consideration that many developing countries do not have the administrative resources required for extensive or detailed regulation and control; and that even where such resources do exist, it is often difficult to ensure that regulation and control are exercised in the interests of the public at large and not merely in the interests of the regulators and controllers. But that does not mean that developing countries

should do away with all controls — only that they should limit themselves to those key controls that they are able to operate efficiently.

As noted earlier, one way of enhancing the efficiency of the controls is to use a simple, structured tariffication. Protection could also be designed to be time bound and performance based to promote enterprise and ensure that excessive protection does not become a way of life. Furthermore, infant-industry protection should be undertaken cautiously in small economies so that economies of scale and division of labour can be exploited. This protection can be set up, for example, by mutual lowering of trade tariffs among similar economies that at the same time maintain or even raise tariffs against the more advanced economies or by subsidizing exports in the early phase.

SUPPLY-SIDE MEASURES AS A FOUNDATION FOR COMPETITIVENESS

A nascent industrializing country would need policies to develop the hard and soft infrastructure required to build up a competitive industrial sector. This would involve massive investment in such hard infrastructure as roads, ports, competitive telecommunication and postal services, electricity, and water supply. Human-capital development through investment in education at all levels, especially in science and technology (S&T) and research and development (R&D), would serve to provide the country with the requisite skills to compete in the modern world. The soft infrastructure would include the institutional framework for doing business — an efficient and transparent regulatory framework, enforcement of contracts and well-defined property rights, insurance and accounting services, development of the money and capital markets, forging of business–government relationships, and so forth.

Furthermore, a range of tax, credit, and labour policies would be needed to lower the operating costs of firms. Institutions to provide long-term finance and procure information relating to technologies and markets need to be designed. Perhaps one of the areas in which government–business relationships would need to be strengthened in Africa relates to the processing of information on foreign markets and technologies. What is proposed here is that the government become actively involved in solving many of the subtle issues related to market access overseas by turning to aggressive economic diplomacy (Soludo 1993). In part, this requires dealing with such mundane matters as reorienting diplomacy so that the most important criterion a country uses for assessing the success of its ambassadors is the extent to which they create a market opening for their country's exports and attract foreign businesses and investment to their own country. This would require innovations in fostering a stronger business–government symbiotic relationship capable of augmenting the market.

ACTIVE TECHNOLOGY POLICY

One consequence of the aversion that proponents of orthodox SAPs have to industrial policy is that these programs proceed without a statement of technological policy. Industrialization of the less industrialized countries in Africa will have to take place under conditions of accelerating technical change and the pervasive application of new technologies. This supports a conceptualization of technological change that emphasizes learning and the accumulation of technological capabilities. Such learning is certainly a public good. This is bound to have considerable implications for the conceptualization of the industrialization problem in Africa.

This approach to industrialization is consistent with the thrust of recent trade and growth models that have focused more explicitly on the microfoundations of innovation by addressing firm-level decisions to invest in product or process innovations. Case studies of exporting firms in six countries showed that a ceaseless search for improvements in technology (especially product quality and cost-lowering process innovations) was most instrumental in improving productivity (Wangwe and Semboja 1998). Productivity growth, in turn, was a most important factor enabling exporting firms to succeed in the changing technological and market conditions. Exporting firms maintained or improved their market position by investing in technology and continuing to improve on it. Improvements were made in the production process to cope with pressure to keep costs at competitive levels or to improve product quality (level and consistency). These changes were made in response to signals given in export markets.

A major implication of the experience of industrial development in Africa is that, in conceptualizing the industrialization problem in Africa, policymakers will need to recognize the ways technological change is occurring. What is needed is an emphasis on learning and the accumulation of technological capabilities within firms, with the requisite support from the state in the form of supportive infrastructural investments. This contrasts with the previous emphasis on the transfer of the capital and know-how required for an industrialization process directed primarily at import substitution. The changing characterization of innovation, the nature of technological change, and the centrality of technological change in trade and international competitiveness mean that the conceptualization of the industrialization problem needs to change accordingly.

Tangential to the supply-side measures is a need for active technology policies relating to the acquisition and adaptation of foreign technology, technical extension, standardization and quality control, the role of transnational corporations in technological development, R&D, assistance in the purchase of foreign technology, and so forth.

The summary lesson from all this is that in a world of imperfect, defective, or missing markets and a weak technological and industrial base, the task of enabling industries to grow and compete is more complex than the SAP model suggests. Rather than asking the government to get out of the way, a realistic model would require active and strategic government participation to make the liberalization process consistent with the country's initial conditions and long-term development goals.

In current policy-making, the industrial sector interacts very little with the technological infrastructure that exists in many countries to provide R&D and technical support to enterprises. Because many of the research institutes are poorly funded, they have inadequate equipment and insufficiently motivated staff. Thus, they do not aggressively search for or offer solutions to the technical problems of industry, preferring instead a more isolated existence. Much the same applies to technological information services set up to help local firms locate and purchase foreign technologies.

The development of the S&T infrastructure and the provision of technical extension services to industry, especially to SMEs, are important supply-side measures that would enable firms to respond to incentives. S&T infrastructure is needed for such basic services as quality control, metrology, R&D, collection and dissemination of information on sources of technology, and assistance in the purchase of foreign technology. It is important to note that quality-control requirements have changed in the past two decades, and international trade in manufactured products increasingly requires stringent proof of quality management of capital. This is of particular importance with the increased stress on privatization and the expectation that private capital — foreign and domestic — will play a central role in the economic recovery and growth of African economies. Economic reforms in many countries in Africa have involved restructuring of public enterprises, a process that has been associated with dramatic changes in ownership structure, capital structure, employment, investment in technology, business-support systems, and marketing strategies. The shift in favour of privatization and private-sector development is quite significant.

Financing industrialization

Investment and financing of industrialization pose new challenges for domestic resource mobilization. The role of the state will be very instrumental in this process, as the experience of some East Asian countries suggests. The history of industrialization reveals a dynamic correspondence between the nature and strategy of industrialization and the financial sectors. Among the latecomers, financial arrangements were created that differed substantially from those of the pioneers of industrialization.

In France and Germany, for instance, the functions of industrial banks were different from the traditional functions of commercial banks. Not limiting their assets to short-term notes of business firms, they invested heavily in long-term obligations and equities of industrial companies. Even more significantly, this allowed them to closely supervise and monitor their clients. In Japan, Zaibatsu played a similar role. The governments of Japan, Korea, and Taiwan provided fiscal support to facilitate investments by reducing the effective tax rate on corporate income, allowing new firms to retain a higher share of profits, and providing investment tax credits. Financial incentives were given in the form of low and stable interest rates, preferential policy loans, and priority allocations of credit and foreign exchange. Competition policy is geared toward productivity and capital accumulation, which sometimes restrict competition and sometimes promote it.

The point here is that financial institutions were included in the industrialization strategies and the industrial structure that emerged. The SAPs, having no specific industrialization policy and premised on an ideology that is antithetical to strategic thinking about industrialization, have essentially decoupled financial policy from industrial policy. More specifically, the issue of development banks must be reexamined to see what role they can play in resource mobilization and allocation.

We have argued for a strategy that encourages both import-substituting and export industries. It is important to indicate the financial requirements of such a strategy, especially if it is to generate an investment–export nexus that leads to diversification of exports. No such investment–export nexus is discernible in the current wave of financial liberalization and adjustment, partly, of course, because according to these orthodox theories, industrial policy or any strategic thinking by the state is anathema. All is supposed to happen automatically. The Asian experience suggests quite clearly that the path embarked on by African countries was inherently contradictory. Stiglitz and Uy (1996) argued that the availability of positive but controlled real interests, ensured by financial restraint or mild financial repression, and credit allocations favouring export sectors were key to the success of the export strategies. Arguing that a market-oriented financial system could not have supported the export-promotion policies pursued by South Korea and Taiwan, Park (1993) advanced a "big-push argument" for a coordinated investment program to exploit complementary externalities and economies of scale. He noted, however, that because the rates of return on investment will differ from sector to sector at an early stage of industrialization, a deregulated financial system is highly unlikely to be able to support such a coordinated investment program without government intervention. In the Asian experience, an investment–export nexus in which government policy was central is discernible. Clearly, in these cases the overriding reason for government intervention in finance in Korea and Taiwan was an industrial policy that promoted exports of manufactures (Park 1993).

The message here is that the shift of credit toward export-oriented activities cannot be expected to be automatic. Long-term capital at reasonable rates of interest is needed for those engaged in export activities. Development financial institutions and restraints are needed to support productive sectors identified as the engines of growth. We therefore need to reexamine development banking, an institutional arrangement that is under heavy assault in Africa, sometimes from institutions that are themselves based on the rationale of development banking as a generic form of ensuring long-term finance for activities the private sector might find too risky.

State and domestic capital

One of the unresolved questions in much of Africa is the relationship between the state and domestic capital. The relationship between government and the enterprise sector influences cooperation with the enterprise sector and the effectiveness of government policy. For many historical reasons, domestic capital in Africa remains weak and by design or default, has, in many cases, been a creation of the state. In few countries are there systematic cooperation and consultation between the state and domestic capitalists. Indeed, in many countries, including those where the official ideology proclaims capitalism, there has been political aversion to the emergence of a relatively independent domestic capitalist class. The normal situation in Africa is one of mutual distrust and recrimination, with state officials accusing the private sector of being parasitic and lethargic and the private sector complaining that the government is corrupt and inefficient. The SAPs have compounded these problems by making states more accountable to funders than to domestic economic interests. Effectively, this means that any pact between the state and local capitalists is secondary to that between the state and international financial institutions. If the latter are afraid of the capture of policy by domestic capitalists, the domestic capitalists have, on their side, to contend with the capture of policy by foreign institutions. The secrecy surrounding policy-making further adds to the sense of insecurity and uncertainty of the private sector. One should recall here that aid constitutes an important determinant of public investment, which crowds out private investment. Private investors' uncertainty about the flows of aid, their patterns, and their sectoral allocation is one of the constraints on private investment. It is surprising how donors are totally oblivious to the presence of private investors and never consider the impact that aid might be having on the decisions of the private sector in Africa. Obviously, strategies calling for higher levels of both public and private investment have to address relations between the state, domestic capital, and foreign capital.

Most governments have accepted privatization of their enterprises, although perhaps not as enthusiastically as the BWIs would like. The privatization process has been slower than expected, partly because of the political implications of the process and partly because private investors, like all others, have not found the policy environment sufficiently stable to warrant long-term investment. Although privatization often means a reduction in the role of the state, privatization itself is a state policy involving fattening of the calf before selling, financing, regulating, and so forth. It, therefore, presupposes the state's capacity to privatize, if the process is not to turn out as a mere looting of the state by those with access to the state's assets. Both the weakness of domestic capital and the predisposition of the state have meant that privatization has been tantamount to denationalization. Governments have failed to use privatization policy, in combination with various state initiatives, to promote a national entrepreneurial base by supporting a nascent capitalist class. This would involve selective protection of the domestic market, joint ventures with foreign capital, selective divestiture with preferential treatment for domestic investors, and support for the export efforts of national industry. It would also require an institutional climate that promotes strategic cooperation between the state, capital, and labour and provides a firm basis for economic policy. A strong domestic capitalist class is not necessarily a threat to foreign capital. Indeed, the existence of such "national bourgeoisie" (rather than the vaunted "well-defined" property rights) is the only guarantee that private property will have political anchoring at the national level. It guarantees politically sustainable and credible property relations. The relationship between foreign and local investment can be made complementary, especially if foreign investment can augment local technological capabilities.

The positive role of foreign investment in building local technological capabilities has come out quite clearly in Mauritius, where local private capital has been progressively buying out foreign capital. This harmonious nationalization of investments has been facilitated by the existence of an entrepreneurial class that developed from the local plantocracy during the years when sugar production was dominant. The surpluses accumulated then were invested in industry. In addition, the macroeconomic environment and the climate for investment have been conducive to both local and foreign investment. Outsiders (foreign firms in some form of partnership with local firms or nonindigenous entrepreneurs) have sometimes been instrumental in initiating the process of building up the capabilities needed to improve competitiveness. This has occurred where these outsiders were incorporated into the national accumulation process, and their capital and know-how were transferred to others (Wangwe 1995). The case studies of six African countries (Wangwe and Semboja 1998) revealed an array of relationships between foreign capital and local capital. In some cases, foreign investment preceded investment by local firms, but the local firms developed and gradually took over ownership of foreign-controlled firms. Foreign investment and other industrialization agents have a role in building technological capabilities. Foreign investment, in particular, could fill some important gaps in the capabilities of African firms. The role of government policy is important in influencing the outcome of those relationships. It should be emphasized that foreign investment will only be beneficial if it is embedded within a broad national strategy driven by the exigencies of a national vision. The presence of such a national vision also makes policy credible to would-be investors.

Human capital as a prerequisite for industrialization

Technological learning does not occur in isolation. It involves interactions with other firms and institutions. Apart from physical inputs, it calls for various new skills, developed in the educational system and training institutes; technical information and services; contract-research facilities; interactions with equipment suppliers and consultants; and standards-regulating bodies. Special skills must be developed to set up this dense network of cooperation.

Economic reforms do not usually address any of the skills shortages that may be affecting the efficiency of African industry, yet many existing industries might become competitive if their human resources were improved. We noted how the SAPs have in many ways undermined the augmentation of broad-based and specialized human capital by their reliance on an essentially static analysis of human-capital returns and needs. Only recently, the dire shortage of critical skills and personnel in Africa has been recognized as an impediment to policy implementation and industrialization. We must not lose sight of the fact that much of the so-called lack of capacity in Africa is donor imposed. How can capacity develop when much of the financial aid is tied to technical assistance, which ensures that much of the money goes to pay foreign advisers who have turned Africa into laboratories for testing their pet theories about development? It is becoming a joke that there will soon be more foreign experts in Africa than there are Africans for them to advise. Some analysts estimate that nearly 40% of the multilateral aid and financial assistance is spent on foreign experts, and about 4 billion USD goes annually to fund foreign technical assistance in Africa. If such an amount were used for training programs, R&D, technological upgrading, and diversification of production structures, Africa's human-capital situation would certainly be different.

Human capital belongs to the realm of externalities for which there are solid theoretical foundations for a more active state role at all levels. It is also an area of great uncertainty for private and public investors in education because of the rapidly changing nature of demand. However, higher levels of education enhance a country's social capacity to adjust to changes. Rather than getting bogged down in rather meaningless calculations of rates of returns, African countries should learn from the historical experience of other developed and developing countries about the importance of investment in human capital at all levels. In all these experiences, one point is clear: tertiary education has always played a critical role in the process of rapid industrialization. Africa currently lags far behind the rest of the world in this, and it is time to initiate programs to narrow the gap. If one has to make errors with regard to the accumulation of human capital, it is better to make them on the side of excess.

Agrarian revolution and reforms

We have seen that through the entire postcolonial period, the poor performance of African agriculture has poised a sword of Damocles over all development strategies. Africa is the only continent where the growth in per capita food production has been lower than the growth in population. Perhaps the biggest surprise with the SAPs has been their failure to affect agriculture in any significant way. In the Berg report (World Bank 1981), it was clear that agriculture was likely to benefit immediately from the SAPs. Coming after a decade of dramatic failure of World Bank project initiatives of the 1970s, the SAPs were a welcome initiative because they focused on broad macroeconomic policies and promised so much. We already noted how poor the performance has been, even in the success stories.

Long-term growth prospects in Africa will depend on how well agriculture performs. In most countries, agriculture will be a source of foreign exchange and savings. It will also be an important source of inputs for industry and a major contributor to the market for some of the infant industries. The chosen pattern of agrarian transformation will also determine the course of equity in the growth process.

Because of its importance, agriculture has continued to receive policy attention, but it has proven to be the Achilles heel of virtually every strategy for development in Africa. Policies in effect before the SAPs can be said to have killed the goose that laid the golden egg by overtaxing the sector. The SAPs were sold as proagriculture strategies that would reverse the antirural bias of ISI. However, this sector of the program also revealed the failure of the World Bank projects. At one time, around 50% of the projects funded by the World Bank were nonperforming. The conviction that getting the macroeconomics right would elicit the required response proved naive. It became clear that sectoral and microlevel policies were needed to directly address the problems of low productivity and low technological levels in African agriculture. More specifically, increased investment was needed in infrastructure, in extending markets to reduce transaction costs, in increased extension services, and so forth. All these required a much more active state than was allowed for under the SAPs.

Schemes are needed for directing credit to rural producers to encourage technical innovation. This may involve subsidized credit or inputs. One should recall that the Green Revolution in Asia required massive intervention in the markets for credit and agricultural inputs. It also demanded policies that protected agriculture from cheap imported grains dumped from countries that heavily subsidized their own agriculture.

Technological change

African agriculture needed policies to directly address the problems of low productivity and low technological levels in this sector. The SAPs have generally ignored technological constraints on agriculture and have exhibited an optimism about supply responses that can only be attributed to faith. Earlier, we noted the low levels of use of modern inputs in African agriculture. Some African countries can still make substantial gains from drawing on the current technological shelf, but given the ecological diversity of the continent, location-specific R&D will play a central role. Reductions in public expenditure have led to drastic cuts in funding for research. This must be reversed. Dissemination of research results will require comprehensive extension services and financial resources. Here again, we encounter an example of the decoupling of the financial sector from production fundamentals. One aspect of the removal of "financial repression" has been the suppression of rural credit schemes that offered credit at subsidized rates (Ssemogerere 1998). This effectively denies African agriculture a major instrument of agrarian transformation that others have used with success elsewhere. Here again, we must reexamine agricultural development banks and other schemes that specifically set aside funds to provide long-term credit to rural producers in conjunction with technological innovations aimed at improving productivity.

Protecting peasants' access to land

A characteristic feature of African agriculture is the preponderance of smallholders, who usually have communal rights to land. From one point of view, this arrangement is considered a hindrance to agrarian transformation because it leaves property rights undefined and, therefore, blocks the proper functioning of financial markets in which land would serve as important collateral. "Commoditization" of land is, therefore, being pushed as part of a process to unleash the market through schemes of land registration, which are already serving as harbingers of land alienation and concentration in the African countryside. Commoditization is also advanced as ensuring clearly defined property rights to encourage better use of land.

There are many reasons to defend the established arrangement for peasant access to land in Africa. First, there are equity considerations. It is this feature of African agriculture that gives promise to relatively egalitarian strategies of agrarian transformation. Second, land alienation caused by commoditization can be politically destabilizing. Africa is not a continent of classical peasant revolt, partly because of these institutional arrangements. Abrupt incursions of market forces can provoke strife along class and ethnic lines that can undermine any strategy for development. Finally, there is the economic argument. Considerable evidence suggests that, contrary to neoliberal opinion, communal ownership of land does not negatively affect the efficient use of land; that properly defined property rights need not be private; and that many small-scale producers reach levels of efficiency in land and labour use that are superior to those of large-scale farming. It is, therefore, possible to envisage strategies of agrarian change in which peasant access to land is not undermined by land registration and privatization. Countries such as Taiwan have demonstrated that high levels of productivity in agriculture can be attained while land alienation and concentration are legally blocked.

One should note that the relative *inter*household equality ensured by traditional access to land does not guarantee *intra*household equity; more specifically, access by women to land and other inputs and to their share of the products of their labour remains a serious source of inequity, as well as of poverty among women, in rural Africa.

Mobilization of resources

Domestic savings

One outstanding feature of the SAPs is their failure to increase savings to levels that can sustain development. Even in the success stories, savings fell far short of investment. For all the talk of globalization of financial markets, there is a remarkably high correlation between domestic savings and investment in most countries (Feldstein and Horioka 1980; Bayoumi 1990). Consequently, it is unlikely that such resource gaps can be eradicated through external financing. African economies will simply have to increase their levels of savings. We should add here that increased domestic savings is also an important element of economic stability. Interestingly, in Africa and Latin America, where the correlation between savings and investment is lowest, we also find the poorest economic performance and the greatest instability. This confirms that over the past two decades, the developing countries that relied most on foreign savings — defined as the top one-third of countries ranked by the ratio of all capital flows to GDP — tended to have higher inflation, higher fiscal deficits, lower investment, and lower growth than those that relied less on foreign-lending inflows.

Earlier, we noted how the simple reliance on interest rates to mobilize domestic savings is obviously inadequate. There is no clear evidence to suggest that the causality between financial growth and real output growth runs from financial liberalization to financial deepening and then to higher output growth. One remarkable feature of the HPEAs was the extent of financial repression. Indeed, the Asian experience with respect to the financial sectors contradicts the advice given to Africans. With regard to South Korea, Park (1993) identified the following features in its financial policies:

- The predominance of indirect finance in the intermediate credit market, although the business sector has increasingly relied on direct finance;
- The repressive nature of the financial system — even after a decade-long promotion of financial liberalization little has changed, according to many liberalization advocates; and
- The insularity of the financial sector.

All this points to the need for African governments to find ways and means to force up the domestic savings ratio. We already indicated that African countries achieved higher levels of domestic savings in the past. Such levels can be attained again, especially if the debt overhang can be relaxed, allowing the public sector to begin saving as well. Efforts to increase both private and public savings will probably have a much higher payoff than the efforts that have hitherto been devoted to attracting foreign capital, both official and private. African governments must seek ways of mobilizing domestic resources. Forced-savings schemes such as the fully funded pension schemes of Singapore and taxation on luxury consumption goods ("Kaldor tax") should be considered. Some form of financial repression will also have to be tolerated to direct savings and to mobilize capital for long-term development.

For several countries in Africa, strategies are needed to encourage flight capital to return home for investment there. For countries such as Nigeria and Zaire, with several tens of billions of dollars in foreign private bank accounts, any program that attracts back a significant portion could unleash the required momentum for growth in some sectors. Government leadership in providing the necessary incentives, legal guarantees of property rights, and encouragement to these owners of funds (however acquired) would be important. For such amnesty to be credible, the government should enjoy popular support and be empowered by the electorate to grant such amnesty. An amnesty declared by those who constitute the "kleptocracy" would be morally reprehensible and ultimately incredible.

In the long run, high rates of growth can be achieved with lower levels of physical investment because knowledge and economies of scale account for an increasing share of growth; however, at earlier stages of growth, high levels of investments are required for any given level of growth. We noted the failure of the expectation that with the SAPs and unleashing of markets, private investment would blossom and FDI would flow in. Private investment as a ratio of GDP has, on the average, been declining since the reform period started. The image of the entrepreneur raring to go if only unleashed simply overlooked the many non-governmental constraints on the emergence of an African capitalist class — external competition, lack of finance, lack of organizational skills; lack of information about markets, products, and technologies; and so forth. The role of the state will be very instrumental in the process of building such a class of entrepreneurs, as the experience of some East Asian countries suggests. As we discussed earlier (see "Financing industrialization," pp. 107–108), the governments of Japan, Korea, and Taiwan used a variety of policy instruments to provide fiscal support to facilitate investments. This suggests that Africa can meet the challenge of mobilizing resources to finance industrialization without relying on forced savings in agriculture.

Public savings and investment

Austerity has now become the key word. This is often because of the objectives of stabilization and debt repayment. In such a context of stabilization fundamentals, states that generate surpluses while their infrastructure collapses are praised for adopting sound fiscal policy. In a developmental context, austerity in the public sector is viewed as shifting resources toward long-term investment in social and physical infrastructure. The state must aim at producing a budget surplus. It is this surplus that will facilitate the state's assumption of the lead role in the economy without contributing to inflationary pressures. The surplus will also cushion the state's own adjustment to short-term fluctuations. Only when it is in a robust fiscal position can the state invest in those activities that will attract private investment and clearly indicate to the private sector the direction of national priorities.

Therefore, the particular nature of such reforms will depend on national characteristics. For instance, for countries with mineral wealth, the mining industry can be used as the fiscal anchor, generating revenue in hard currency for both stabilization and economic growth. Chile, which is often cited as being neoliberal, seems to have used the state-owned mining industry to service past debts and to generate a fiscal surplus. The state was then able to play an active role in agricultural and industrial policies by using this surplus to grant subsidized public credit and technical assistance to new export-oriented agricultural and industrial activities based on natural resources.

We should caution, however, that surpluses should not be generated cheaply by either senseless and unplanned cuts in public expenditure or distress sales of state enterprises at ridiculously low prices to address short-run fiscal problems. We are urging that public savings be generated from the better performance of the state (including the parastatals), better collection of taxes, and clearer long-term investment programs.

Partly because of the fiscal crisis of the state and the ideological stance that public investment was inherently inefficient and crowded out private investment, public investment has collapsed in Africa. In recent years, it has become abundantly clear that one constraint on private investment is this collapse. The state must revive public investment within a framework of long-term development thinking, not only to guide the private sector toward national priorities but also to develop plans in light of well-articulated state priorities and projects.

In addition, efforts must be made to enhance the capacity of the state to channel public, private, and external savings to finance investments through development banks or specialized investment funds. As Fanelli and Frenkel (1994) argued, carefully administered development banks could efficiently develop screening devices to select private-investment projects. Such an argument is reinforced by the lack of long-term capital markets in most African countries. It is unlikely in Africa that private markets will generate a flow of financial intermediation high enough to support a substantial rate of investment in productive activities. As we stressed, the axiomatic scheme that associates financial liberalization with high savings and then high investment simply does not hold in Africa.

Studies of stock-exchange markets suggest that they are unlikely to finance long-term investments at desirable levels.

External finance

PRIVATE-CAPITAL FLOWS

Several issues emerge from the analysis of the experience with financial liberalization. First, Africa is unlikely to get the kind of capital inflows that will significantly shift the growth path beyond the current low levels. Both the quality and quantity of these inflows make them unlikely to play much of a developmental role.

Second, the design of economic policy on the basis of high expectations for the quantity and quality of foreign capital inflows is likely to lead to failure and incorrect prioritization. Such expectations also generate the kind of distorted emphasis on financial fundamentals that we indicated earlier. Even while it is conceded that the concept of international capital markets as an engine of development has been oversold, it is argued that such capital flows are a vote of confidence for a particular policy. The fact that a country is attracting foreign capital is said to indicate that a country is pursuing the correct economic policy. This, however, may not be true. As we have argued earlier, getting the fundamentals that attract portfolio investments right does not mean that the policy is getting other developmental fundamentals right. Indeed, in many cases, governments introduce fiscal and monetary discipline that leads to high interest rates and currency reevaluation that in turn undermine investment and exports, although this is done in the expectation that their fiscal stance will attract foreign capital.

And, finally, the Latin American experience clearly suggests a need to distinguish between volatile short-term investment and more stable long-term flows such as FDI. Chile introduced a tax on inflows, but such a tax need not be big. Even a small tax is prohibitively expensive for very short-term round-tripping, but it is a negligible cost for long-term investment. It is clear that policy in Africa will have to include measures to deter short-term speculative flows and to prevent excessive exchange-rate appreciation. Evidence from other countries that such policies do discourage the most volatile inflows may actually account for the prominence of FDI in countries such as Chile.

We have discussed the wave of liberalization of financial markets and the rather poor response of foreign capital to the policies of African countries. However, we should not rule out the possibility of sudden spurts in portfolio-investment flows into some countries. The position of African governments has been to make themselves as attractive as possible, the position being that beggars cannot be choosers. The view under the SAPs seems to be that because there is no massive inflow of portfolio investment, there is no point fussing about managing inflows. One should then literally be content with whatever comes one's way. However, this attitude of African states toward unregulated financial markets is self-defeating. The short-term inflows are there to arbitrage interest differentiation or to obtain quick capital gains. Usually such flows cause sharp increases in domestic asset prices and unsustainable exchange appreciation. Such appreciation conflicts with other objectives of the SAPs, that is, to increase and diversify exports. The instability wrought by such inflows tends to discourage long-term investment. In such circumstances, a state with a policy that suggests complete abandonment of its authority and national priorities will not be credible to serious investors. This means that policymakers must exercise prudence in allowing capital inflows. The current attitude of African governments is not only myopic but also tantamount to shirking of responsibility. Financial flows must be subject to the requirements of an overall strategy for development in the recipient country.

Evidence suggests that if the objective is to attract FDI, then the appropriate policies would be ones that restrict the inflows of "hot money" and create a favourable climate for long-term investment by enhancing social and political stability and providing physical infrastructure and a skilled labour force. Creating such an enabling environment requires a much more proactive state than is usually the case. The largest recipient of FDI has been China, which has maintained restrictions on capital flows and maintained extensive state ownership. What is actually needed is a clear, transparent, and predictable policy of controls and incentives for capital inflows. Such a program must signal the preference for FDI and an aversion for short-term speculative inflows that destabilize the economy. This assures those with long-term investment plans that the government's intention is to provide a stable environment for such long-term investment.

AID

Besides increased domestic savings and repatriated flight capital, another potential source of resources for investment is external aid. Aid inflow increased from 3.4% of GNP in 1980 to 16.3% of GNP in 1995 in SSA (World Bank 1997). Although many African countries depend on aid to fund even the most basic of government programs, its overall impact on the economies of the region has been questioned. According to Sachs (1996, p. 20), "foreign aid, notoriously, has not made much difference in Africa. It has sometimes delayed reform and has sometimes been irrelevant." Sachs argued that aid has become a way of life for many countries and that IMF–World Bank programs rarely constitute a strategy for initiating growth in Africa. *Adjustment in Africa* (World Bank 1994) may have been correct in arguing that net resource flows to Africa have been positive over the reform period, but it is obviously wrong to argue that as a consequence, external-debt servicing has not constituted a drag on African development. First, such aggregate data mask the individual country experiences; and, second, they create the illusion that it is the mere magnitude, as opposed to the purpose, of such inflows that affects growth.

The fact that investment is falling in the region despite the positive net resource inflow indicates that it could be the composition of flows, rather than their magnitude, that matters more for growth. Yes, Africa has received more aid per capita than any other region, but this aid, which is often for balance-of-payment purposes or is tied to the interests of the donors, contributes very little to growth — as the saying goes, "he who pays the piper calls the tune." It is Africa's aid dependence that has given foreign institutions so much power in African national affairs. And their capacity to impose SAPs reflects this. Aid dependence has reached the point where it is counterproductive, as it seems to do nothing to generate processes that would obviate the need for it. The aid–recipient relationship in Africa has developed into one that neither generates mutual respect nor synergetically harnesses the capacities of all those involved. Instead, it has generated the dependency syndrome, cynicism, and "aid fatigue."

The capacity of aid institutions in the new economic dispensation needs to be addressed. Few of the aid institutions (including the World Bank) have a track record in assisting the growth of a dynamic private sector, aid having been largely a government-to-government affair. There is, therefore, the danger that as these aid institutions shift their resources to the private sector, they may impart to the private sector the same aid dependence, rent seeking, and lethargy as they imparted to state institutions. Any serious strategy for development must reexamine the aid–development nexus.

For their part, African countries ought to abandon their supine position. They need to more precisely define what external assistance they require, based on clearly defined national goals and an exhaustive mobilization of national capacities and resources. For most countries to move forward, it is imperative that both the donors and the recipients seriously rethink the purpose and nature of aid to Africa. No doubt, some aid plays some positive role, but policymakers should initiate a major debate about the potential for channeling aid in a manner that enhances the building and use of African human resources, mobilizes domestic resources, and weans African economies away from an aid dependence that simply does nobody any good.

Reducing the debt

Perhaps the most important constraint on the resumption of growth in Africa is the external-debt overhang. SSA, with 26 of the 32 developing countries that are classified as highly indebted poor countries (HIPCs), is the most debt-distressed region in the world. In about a decade, despite the positive net resource inflows and revolving debt-relief schemes (including refinancing), the SSA could only service one-third of its obligations. Debt stock has been rising explosively (mainly as a result of capitalization of unpaid interest arrears and amortization), and a large number of countries have been classified as simply insolvent.

The consequences of debt overhang to the macroeconomy are monumental, and meaningful growth is unlikely to resume without a resolution to the debt crisis. Elbadawi et al. (1996) recently produced a highly insightful study. They estimated the effects of debt overhang on African economies and also assessed the adequacy of the recent multilateral debt initiative for HIPCs. The channels through which debt overhang translates into a drag on growth are multifaceted. First, the rising debt-service ratios (in the face of rapidly growing debt stock) reduce the availability of resources for initiating growth. Second, in the face of stagnating exports, rising debt-service payments have entailed either payment defaults or a drain on scarce foreign exchange needed to import production inputs. Growth is the victim, and this exacerbates the solvency problem. Both the internal and the external transfer constraints on debt service are severe, but the internal transfer is worsened by the growing depreciation of the local currencies in seemingly stagnant economies. In servicing their external debt, most countries have been put in extremely distressed fiscal positions; the result is severely compressed development budgets and a shrinking fiscal base for essential public services. Thus, all the proposals for a functional or developmentalist state, which is necessary for initiating and supporting growth-inducing activities, are constrained by a shrinking resource base. Little scope is left in the area of expenditure reduction or restructuring, as aggressively mobilized revenues (amounting to increased private-sector transfers) end up being used for debt servicing. Furthermore, the debt burden creates uncertainty about the credibility and sustainability of reforms and constitutes a potential threat to investment. Investors either refrain from committing irreversible capital investment or are content with short-term investment in trading activities.

Under these circumstances, Elbadawi et al. (1996, p. 3) suggested that "stabilization by itself may not be enough to trigger the 'good equilibrium' which is consistent with a virtuous circle — from stabilization to growth." On the basis of cross-sectional regressions for 99 developing countries spanning Africa, Asia, Latin America, and the Middle East, the authors argued (Elbadawi et al. 1996, p. 20) that

> The debt burden faced by the African HIPCs has very strongly and negatively affected economic growth since the second half of the 1980s; threatened the sustainability of reforms; and prevented the development of a capable and functional state, due to the fiscal crisis that ensued. And despite the adequacy of the guidelines, the Multilateral debt initiative may, in effect, end up being inadequate for propelling SSA to the minimum growth path required for reversing its current economic decline. Moreover, when the model-based criteria [are] applied for classifying the debt situation of African countries, the set of "unsustainable" HIPCs is found to be much larger than indicated by the IMF/WB [World Bank] classification.

This analysis and empirical evidence reinforce what most analysts of the African crisis have stressed on many occasions: that resuming long-run sustainable growth in Africa would be extremely difficult, if not impossible, without addressing the debt overhang. Alternative solutions to the crisis have adorned the literature, and each one has its own costs and benefits. However, several analysts would agree with Sachs (1996, p. 21) that "the assistance should come in the form of debt cancellation. No one can doubt the dreadful policy errors of the past, nor the mutual complicity of African and donor nations. A fresh start requires a thick line drawn under the past."

This solution, simple as it sounds, holds the key to Africa's future. All efforts to find out why stabilization or adjustment has not worked, why investment has not resumed, and why the state capacity has been further eroded will fail unless this single but dominant issue — debt overhang — is included. What is needed is either an immediate solution to this crisis or the articulation of a comprehensive reform program for sustaining growth despite the debt.

Regional integration

We noted that among the fundamentals to be addressed is the question of markets. Rather than passively waiting for the "invisible hand" to determine the course of events, successful developmental states have created or governed markets. Also, they have sought strategic integration into global markets in ways that enhance national goals. A recurring theme in the pan-African debate on economic policy and development is regional integration. The case for regional administration and the difficulties and failures encountered in trying to implement regional-integration schemes are recounted in many places and need not detain us here. What is salient is that right from the beginning, with the publication of the Berg report (World Bank 1981), the SAP was juxtaposed against a vision of regional integration — the Lagos Plan of Action. The Berg report carried the day, however, and debate on regional integration must now be carried out in the context of the SAPs.

Perhaps a fundamental difference between the SAPs and the regional-integration model is that whereas the latter is based on an explicit articulation of an industrial policy, the SAPs have generally eschewed the statement of industrial policy beyond the extension of the liberalization doctrine to industry itself. In particular, outward orientation in the context of the SAPs calls for unilateral reduction and rationalization of protection. The regional-integration model assumes that a certain degree of protection is required for industry within the region. Oyejide (1996) noted that at the aggregate level, Africa's global and production-oriented approach to regional integration reflects its attempt to create regional economies more independent of the world economy — to insulate them from international shocks — while also promoting overall economic development through an inward-oriented ISI strategy based on protected regional (and hence larger) markets. As Oyejide further noted (1996, pp. 19–20),

> The two tendencies are obviously inconsistent and cannot co-exist permanently. It is clear that unilateral trade liberalisation measures taken by individual countries under SAP effectively reduce the degree of preference enjoyed by regional partners in an integrated area. More significantly, these measures are typically articulated and implemented at [the] national level without reference to any existing or envisaged obligations under specific RIs [regional integrations].

Debate on regional integration concentrates much more on complementarities than it does on product differentiation and competition within the larger market. There is a need to move away from the extreme emphasis on complementarities to a recognition that within the various regional schemes an array of products already exists that could be the basis for competitive markets. Regional arrangements can be used as a collective agency of restraint. In addition, regional integration could serve the dual function of extending and deepening import substitution and promoting exports and Africa's competitiveness in global markets. Forms of regional integration that are protective from the point of view of the rest of the world but that allow and encourage competition within the boundaries could serve as training grounds for industries of the region preparing for global markets.

Sociopolitical fundamentals

Problems of unemployment and economic stagnation have revived interest in economic growth and the explanations behind the differences in the performance of economies. This interest has refocused attention on the nonphysical elements of accumulation, as symbolized by the proliferation of the term *social* in the studies of accumulation. This focus is expressed variously as "social capital," "social capability," and the "social structure of accumulation." What all these terms suggest is that the capabilities embodied in human beings and in the social arrangements that human beings establish play a central role in accumulation and economic development. These capabilities and their embodiments include the technical skills needed to handle the physical hardware of investment; organizational skills; social arrangements that reduce moral hazards or transaction costs in general; creation and governance of markets; social relations in the workplace that guide management–labour relations; state–society relationships; political arrangements that guarantee stability; and institutions that define property relations. They also include ideological positions; social attitudes; cultural determinants of thrift; and consumption patterns along class, gender, and ethnic lines. The range of things included may seem so unwieldy that it makes the concept itself meaningless, but a holistic view of the development process demands that they all be included. In the current debate, much of this has been collapsed under the rubric of governance. Unfortunately, the technocratic twist given to the idea of governance makes it a rather poor summary of these social concerns.

In most cases, orthodox fundamentals are formulated and implemented without taking into account the demands of good governance. Policies that threaten stability or the authority of elected bodies are introduced in isolation, without consideration of the exigencies of governance. Both the economic crisis and the chosen way of resolving it have undermined governmental effectiveness in Africa and reinforced the erosion of the state's political capacity to construct and maintain a working political coalition capable of sustaining the implementation of state policy. Of even greater saliency is that this threatens the process of democratization under way in many African countries. A major assumption we put forth here is that economic policy must, in content and in form, be compatible with and promote the processes of democratization for at least three reasons:

- The intrinsic value we place on democracy and the need to nurture and support it under what are obviously not the most auspicious conditions for its emergence in a number of countries;
- The feeling that Africa's social pluralism and history are such that only a democratically elected government stands a chance of managing these diversities (the search for national and continental unity through repression of diversity has proven ultimately futile and extremely costly in Africa); and
- Third, the need for a government to have enough strength, in terms of technical capacity, political legitimacy, and social anchoring, to carry out the programs suggested here.

We stress the importance of such sociopolitical fundamentals because the failure to have them in place can completely scuttle any sound economic policy. Africa abounds with examples of countries that impressed donors with their "sound" economic policies while their political systems were on the verge of collapse. The most recent case is Burundi, which was considered a strong adjuster. The World Bank (1994, p. 11), in an embarrassing lapse of political sense (as subsequent events were to demonstrate), stated,

> Despite the initial difficulties, Burundi's adjustment program has been path-breaking and should be deemed successful if only in the sense that for the first time it introduced the notions and practice of more effective macroeconomic management. Indeed, fundamental change is under way in Burundi. Taken as a whole, the business climate in Burundi has improved markedly in recent years.

Developmental states, once again

No one would disagree that the fundamental challenge of the postadjustment era will be to develop strategies for rapid capital accumulation and growth propelled by massive private and public investment. To tie up all these fundamentals into some coherent whole, one needs a theory of development that delineates the role of the state. The advocates of the SAPs do not have a coherent theory of growth or a theory of the ways stabilization and liberalization are linked to the rate of growth. The problem, according to Rodrik (1995, p. 938), is that

> Liberalisation is frequently advertised as generating benefits that go far beyond these static gains and it is here that the intellectual underpinning of liberalisation policies are [sic] weakest. This is particularly the case for the oft-repeated benefits in terms of economic growth. Unlike what much current practice leads us to believe, economic theory is generally silent about the effect of liberalisation on the rate of growth of an economy. Since reigning growth is the chief purpose of structural adjustment packages and liberalisation is the central policy tool of such packages, we are left with a discomforting gap between target and instrument.

The neoclassical theory upon which the SAP is constructed is a tightly knit web of assumptions and inferences. It is an impressive edifice of axioms. This axiomatic mode of reasoning pervades much of the policies proposed under the program. On the basis of this axiomatic reasoning, little room was left for the state. A central aspect of development economies has been the breakdown of such axiomatic approaches as a result of market failure.

. The neoclassical orthodoxy that provided the intellectual basis for the SAPs was hostile to active government involvement in economic affairs and completely ignored issues related to institutional development. Over time, revolutions have occurred in ideas about how market economies function, about the scope of government, and about how it can or should function.[2] By far the most virulent assault on government intervention came with the neoclassical resurgence in the 1970s, which was also

---

[2]Stigliz and Uy (1996) succinctly summarized three rounds of such revolutions — from the Walrasian, Arrow–Debreu world of efficient markets; to the neoliberal world of rational expectations, rent-seeking behaviour of public officials, and efficient markets; to the reassessment of markets and reinvention of government championed by the Greenwald and Stigliz (1984, 1986) world of imperfect information and incomplete markets — as well as the East Asian economies' experiences with successful government intervention.

reinforced by the apparent failings of big governments in the Western world and those of socialist economies.

Three sets of theoretical arguments were put forward to justify minimalist government involvement:

- It was argued that anything the government can do the market can do even better — after all, the government faces all the limited-information problems of markets but also faces serious incentive problems because it lacks the profit motive.
- The rational expectations provided a basis for arguing that the government is largely irrelevant — whatever it does, the private sector can or certainly will undo.
- The public-choice literature provided arguments to illustrate the inefficiencies and distorting effects of the rent-seeking behaviour of public officials.

The central message of this view was that even under circumstances of market failure, one cannot rely on the government to remedy the situation — indeed, the government is as likely to be part of the problem as it is to be part of the solution. In the specific context of Africa and the SAPs, the economic crisis was attributed mostly to government failure — misguided policies and pervasive interventions. It was, therefore, not surprising that the major plank of the SAPs was the unleashing of markets, privatization of public enterprises, and general deregulation of the economy.

In more recent years, however, the problems of growth and employment in the developed countries and the stagnation and low economic growth and the obvious role of the interventionist state in the high-performing countries have revived interest in development economics and developmental states. Recent writings have rigorously restated such central concepts of development economics as externalities, endogenous technological learning, asymmetric information, structural rigidities, transaction costs, and the public-good nature of information. Each of these provides a clear theoretical justification for public intervention (Krugman 1992).

This counter counter-revolution, which in fact began during the prime of the neoclassical orthodoxy, has provided a basis for reassessing market failures and once more elevating the prominent role of government. The intellectual precursor to this revolution was provided by Greenwald and Stiglitz (1984, 1986) and the new trade theories (Helpman and Krugman 1985). We should also mention the new growth theories that have revived interest in such topics as economies of scale, human resources, and technology. Greenwald and Stigliz demonstrated that when information is imperfect and markets are incomplete — that is, essentially always — then in principle government intervention can make everyone better off. This theorem forced a change in the debate and a modification of the neoclassical position. Many critics of government had to contend that it was not that markets yielded efficient outcomes, only that government was even worse. In contrast, the new trade theorists have suggested that models incorporating imperfect competition, economies of scale, and learning effects provide a more realistic framework for understanding international trade, intraindustry trade, and specialization. These theories recognize the role of policies in the creation of international competitiveness and in the modification of comparative advantage. In effect, by contradicting the neoclassical models and demonstrating that policies can have effects, depending on how they alter the domestic market structure, the new theories have lent some support to strategic policy interventions. Furthermore, these theoretical insights have been buttressed by the mounting evidence that the much advertised East Asian miracle succeeded mainly because of the governments' abilities to address market failure. Evidence shows that the governments in these economies created markets where they did not exist and provided the institutional infrastructure needed for market development, including a sound regulatory framework.

After nearly two decades of controversy, the balance of opinion tends to suggest that the way forward might well lie at the centre. It is broadly agreed that although the market and private-sector initiatives should be the fulcrum of economic activities, the transformation of most developing countries to higher levels of economic performance cannot occur without a relatively efficient, capable, and willing state. Stiglitz and Uy (1996, p. 268) summarized the debate and pointed the way forward for developing countries by noting that

> Almost by definition, market failures are more prevalent in less developed economies: one of the essential ways in which such countries are less developed is that markets are less developed, and therefore market failures are a more common occurrence. At the same time, government failures are also more prevalent: thus, the ability of government to overcome these market failures is more circumscribed. Ascertaining the appropriate scope of government

entails balancing the limitations of government with the limitations of markets. There is no general theorem asserting that government should have a larger or smaller relative role in earlier or later stages of development, nor even any obvious metric by which such differences might be measured. The East Asian miracle might provide hints about which types of intervention are more likely to be successful or desirable — and how such interventions might be designed ... (i) government is more likely to be effective if it uses, supplements and "governs" markets than if it attempts to replace them; (ii) the government is more likely to be effective if it employs objective performance measures, which not only reduce the scope for corruption, but which, if appropriately chosen, can provide high powered incentives (particularly when performance measures are linked with contests, with well-defined rules and rewards and generally accepted "referees" ensuring that the "game" is played fairly).

The current position is that there are no theoretical reasons why a deliberate and interventionist development policy cannot be pursued. Indeed, both theory and practice provide strong arguments for the kinds of developmentalist interventionism that the most successful economic performers of this century have pursued. This has led the proponents of the antistatist position to shift from purely economic arguments to concerns about institutional factors that allow the capture of state policies by rent-seekers and patronal–clientalist relationships and to concerns about the state's lack of capacity to choose the right things to do. This has opened policy debate to concerns of political economy.

The emerging perspective in favour of greater state involvement draws attention to the capacity of the state to play the developmental roles of steering and nurturing economic activities to desired ends — the Asian way. Besides capacity, three key characteristics of a developmental state include endowment with a professional, disciplined, and skilled central administration; rule that is not by coercion alone but has a broad base of popular legitimacy throughout the national territory; and, finally, a deep political commitment to economic growth (see Gyimah-Boadi and van de Walle 1996).

The argument that government failure can exceed market failures is often specifically aimed at Africa. The recent World Bank (1997) report on the role of the state is typical of such analyses. Conceding that the state has played a central role in the development of Asian countries, the report suggests, time and again, that African states are simply unable to replicate that experience. Most examples of state failure are drawn from the African experience. Most analysts would agree that relative to other regions of the world, the key features of a developmental state are rather thin or weak in Africa. Indeed, what we have witnessed during the economic crisis and adjustment period is the shredding of state institutions, further reducing their developmental capacity. As Aron (1996, p. 117) summarized it,

> The state in Africa has come full circle to the small government of pre-colonial days, but with the additional hysteresis effect from past shocks of a seriously depleted current institutional capability, deterioration in the current quality and scope of social services and infrastructure provision, coupled with a fiscal position highly vulnerable to changes in foreign aid.

Aron highlighted the path-dependent nature of the evolution of institutions and suggested that empirical (endogenous) growth models without comprehensive proxies for initial institutional conditions and shocks to institutions may seriously underestimate the costs of adjusting to new higher growth equilibrium. In the context of the new growth models, therefore, the very weaknesses of African institutions are important determinants of their poor performance, and the past and current weaknesses are being compounded over time. In essence, therefore, unless the problem of state weaknesses is tackled and institutional reforms are undertaken, the resumption of sustained growth is unlikely in much of Africa.

The history and circumstances of Africa's weak states and institutions are too well known to require detailed treatment here (see Shivji 1980; Young 1982; Amin 1987; Anyang Nyong'o 1988; Ake 1990; Callaghy 1990; Bangura 1992; Bayart 1993; Mamdani 1995; Olukoshi 1998). Brautigam (1996), however, summarized the political and historical roots of the problems as follows:

> Most of today's countries were totally new states at independence in the 1960s, and they were given (or won) the mantle of statehood without, in most cases, first building a unified nation. These new states had only a short period of time in which to learn how to manage complex bureaucracies before economic crisis beginning in the middle to late 1970s caused a virtual breakdown of the public sector. Although leadership matters, even the finest leaders can do little without the proper tools and resources, information, managerial and technical expertise, appropriate policy instruments, and finance. Additionally, building capacity is a learning process. It grows with

experience, both of individuals and organisations, and is aided by the institutionalisation of bureaucratic values. State capacity is also shaped by capacity in society and by societal linkages, including policy networks that draw on private sector expertise and other institutions that allow for the embedding or inclusion of societal capacity in the state. Finally, the problem has been exacerbated by the unintended consequences of extensive dependence on foreign aid.

Brautigam defined *state capacity* as a measure of the ability of a government to implement its policies and accomplish its goals. This capacity has four dimensions:

- Regulatory capacity — the ability of the state to establish and enforce the rules that guide or regulate societal behaviour;
- Administrative capacity — the routine ability of the state to manage its own personnel and the resources of the state and to ensure accountability and efficiency in service delivery;
- Technical capacity — the expertise and knowledge required to make and implement technical decisions, whether in science and engineering or in macroeconomics, as well as the policy tools and instruments necessary to implement those decisions effectively; and
- Extractive capacity — the ability of the state to raise the revenues it needs to pay for the implementation of its policies and goals.

Brautigam's (1996) analysis points to the historical roots of weak African states and the current impediments to capacity-building and, more so, hints at some features of the evolutionary process of state strength. Given the current terrain in Africa, some important questions are these: How would such a competent or developmental state emerge or evolve? Who would implement the measures needed for the reconstruction of the state? These are questions to which there are no easy answers. In part, the speed and effectiveness of the reform process would depend on the initial conditions of each country, especially the nature and extent of development of civil society and the state–civil-society relationships; the resource base; and, most important, the emergence of visionary social movements and actors committed to making fundamental changes and to laying the foundations for long-term development.

African countries could learn some important lessons from some Asian experiences in institution-building. Although Asia is widely different in terms of the long history of its evolution, national development, and constellation of the cultural, historical, and external and domestic threats that made the evolution of such models imperative and conducive, Africans could learn from the structural characteristics of the models. Each African state would then need to adapt the relevant institutions to its own sociocultural and historical context.

Initial analysis of the developmental states tended to emphasize the autonomy of the policymakers and their insulation from societal pressures. Such a view stemmed from the essentially authoritarian character of the leading developmental states. And until quite recently, advice to African countries was, therefore, that they should also seek political regimes with such characteristics.

A major lesson from the Asian experiences, however, is that state capacity must not be seen merely in terms of the prowess and perspicacity of technocrats within the state apparatus, but in terms of a durable and effective institutional structure. More significantly, a developmental state must be socially anchored, and its autonomy must be embedded in the social fabric that constitutes a nation. That is the message from much of the revisionist right about the Asian experience (see, for instance, Evans 1992). Such states, according to Evans (1992, p. 154), combine

> Weberian bureaucratic insulation with intense immersion in the surrounding social structure. How this contradictory combination is achieved depends, of course, on both the historically determined character of the state apparatus and the nature of the social structure in which it is embedded.

Key elements of this model are worth emphasizing. First, it confirms the Weberian requirements of a coherent, meritocratic, and disciplined bureaucracy. Second, it notes that such capacity should not be equated with insulation but can be exercised in a dynamic interaction with the external ties and surrounding social structure. In the specific case of Japan, some analysts emphasize this point by arguing that the state's effectiveness emerges not from its inherent capacity but from the complexity and stability of its interaction with market players. In some sense, too, embeddedness can provide some solution to the shortage of capacity. It is particularly necessary because policies must respond to the perceived problems of the private sector and ultimately rely on private actors for implementation. In essence, such a concrete network of ties reinforces the state's capacity by providing it with first-hand opportunities to assess, monitor, and shape private responses to policy initiatives, both before and after the fact. This kind of interaction thus extends the state's intelligence and increases the likelihood that policies will be implemented.

From the foregoing it is evident that a major challenge in transforming the African state into a developmental one is to go beyond merely enhancing its technobureaucratic capacity and seek to embed such a developmental state within democratic social institutions and governance frameworks. This major challenge requires imagination and a sense of history. Indeed, the constitution of democratic developmental states may be the single most important task on the policy agenda in Africa. Such a process is not facilitated by the current practice that removes key elements of economic policy from democratic scrutiny by placing them in the hands of an insulated technocracy (Mkandawire 1996).

Toward democratic governance

Policy-making is a fundamental political process, despite the main attempts to reduce it to a purely technical activity. What Africa does not need is more "good" governance like that defined in the narrow, technocratic, functionalist terms meant to further the goals of an adjustment model that is as controversial as it is contested. What Africa does need is a system of democratic governance in which political actors have the space to freely and openly debate, negotiate, and design an economic-reform package that is integral to the construction of a new social contract for ushering Africa into the 21st century.

Africa's postadjustment strategy for economic reform and democratic governance must include economic-policy measures that are based on a domestic social contract and strengthen, rather than undermine, fragile democratic institutions and processes in need of consolidation. With such a strategy, Africa should be able to overcome the failings and shortcomings of the pre- and postpolitical reform, orthodox adjustment years. The need for the policy measures to be sensitive to the social and welfare aspirations of the populace cannot be overemphasized. Few doubt that drastic measures need to be carried out to reform African economies and polities. However, such drastic measures stand a better chance of success if they are built into a negotiated social contract in which various interest groups have a stake. The contract will also provide a framework within which state and governmental legitimacy can be reconstructed for formulating and implementing policies. Groups are not inherently averse to making sacrifices, including taking cuts in their consumption levels, if they are satisfied that these are temporary measures carried out within the boundaries of a negotiated social contract in which they are stakeholders.

Developing a social contract at this time will require a concerted attack on policy-making traditions and structures that are part and parcel of current authoritarianism on the continent. At one level, this will involve efforts to dismantle the authoritarianism that permeates both governance and donor–recipient relations. At another level, it will entail the recovery by domestic-policy and political forces of the initiative for reform design and implementation, as sanctioned through democratic institutions and processes. Furthermore, it will need closer attention to the impact of economic-reform instruments and policies and a recognition of the limits of the state's political capacity, as dictated by the balance of social forces. It is precisely because of the failure to come to terms with these factors, on the one hand, and the attempt to manage them out of existence, on the other, that the quest for democratic governance in Africa is so elusive.

Strengthening the fiscal capacity of the state

By subordinating fiscal policy to the exigencies of stabilization, the SAPs have undermined the developmental role of fiscal policy. Focus has been on reducing expenditures to remove the deficit and to essentially rein in the state, either because it crowded out the private sector or because it was inherently inefficient. Also, when attention was paid to the allocation of public expenditure, the general view was that all this would take place at lower levels of public expenditure. Focus on deficit reduction through cuts in public expenditure has meant that less attention has been paid to taxation issues.

The new thrust in fiscal policy must be to restore the developmental role of both public expenditure and taxation. Public revenue must be increased to enable the state to meet the exigencies of stabilization and investment. The strategy will need a two-pronged approach:

- Rationalization of public expenditure to make it more focused on developmental fundamentals and to reduce waste; and
- Tax reform to increase state revenue, to ensure more equitable tax collection, and to provide incentives for investment and growth.

Reforming the civil service

African administrative structures were inherited from the former colonial powers. Such structures had served the minimum functions of colonial control and had been insulated from the colonized peoples. In the post-colonial phase, the state assumed a much broader range of activities and policy agendas and had a much wider reach than its colonial predecessor. This made the state more amenable to societal pressures and more open to clientalistic relationships. The need to reform African administrative structures to ensure efficiency and reduce the likelihood of corruption is obvious.

Current initiatives to reform the civil service are based on a crust of suspicion and an essentially cynical view of public servants. As a result, the emphasis is on retrenchment, monitoring, and control, rather than on long-term, sustainable "right-sizing" and performance arrangements, worker discretion, and autonomy.

Among the damaging legacies of the SAP framework that will take time to repair are

- The mistaken idea that civil-service retrenchment is the same thing as reform;
- The diminished real wages for public employees and the consequent loss of morale;
- The resulting brain drain that depleted the civil service of its capacity; and, most important,
- The loss of confidence suffered by employees of the civil service and other governmental agencies, who were constantly berated because they were perceived as being the constraints on development.

Under the SAPs, all the economic ills were attributed to the "poor policies" of the past, and the public servants were severely ridiculed for incompetence, lack of capacity, and proclivity for rent-seeking activities. The policy direction was massive retrenchment, combined with a deluge of foreign advisers, consultants, and representatives of multilateral agencies who took over key policy-analysis and policy-making institutions in many African states. The result, if anything, has been further demoralization and disillusionment. How anybody expected the remaining civil servants to be committed to implementing policies mostly designed in Washington beats the imagination.

The first point of reform in the civil service should be to address issues of capacity, and the emphasis should be on reconstruction rather than on retrenchment. The fact is that since the 1980s a succession of fiscal-stabilization programs and expenditure cuts has reduced government employment in Africa to the lowest level of any developing region

(Schiavo-Campo 1996). The central goal of the reform should be to create a skilled and efficient government work force. This would entail significant reorganization and modernization to make the civil service sensitive and responsive to the modern-day requirements of development. Redundant agencies and operations should be scrapped, and several duplications of functions could be rationalized. The high point of the reform should involve mechanisms for constant retraining and retooling of personnel with new ideas and administrative technologies. Some critical government agencies — especially the customs department, the revenue-mobilization agency, and the ports authority — might need fundamental overhaul. This overhaul would have to be done in tandem with the reform of the overall tax structure and administration. Furthermore, no meaningful and sustainable reform can occur without ensuring that the service can attract and retain highly qualified and competent personnel. The issue of a competitive wage structure to reward competence comes to the fore.

The second aspect of the reform, which is more subtle, pertains to rebuilding a damaged esprit de corps and the lost confidence of bureaucrats. The remaining civil servants, who were for several years derided in most policy analyses and pronouncements as being the cause of the problem, would now be reoriented to become the vanguard of developmental ideals. Completely wiping out the old system with a view to starting afresh might in the end be counterproductive. This would lead to permanent loss of capacity. For the benefit of retaining some institutional memory, it is important to transform the bureaucracy into one that is developmental by, at least initially, reorienting the mentality and the accumulated skills and experience of the bureaucrats. The issues of remuneration and recognition would need to be addressed, and the bureaucrats would need a redefinition of their roles in development. An important ingredient of this reorientation would be to allow bureaucrats to reclaim from foreign experts the authority to initiate, formulate, and implement policies. The only way for them to develop these skills is to grow on the job — making mistakes and learning as they go along but within the overall context of the development agenda. This is the message from examples of successful reforms in other developing countries (Tendler 1997).

Programs for capacity-building and use

A sustainable civil-service reform requires mechanisms for continuous generation and use of new ideas and new personnel. This requires investment in educational training and research and, particularly, the development of, and interaction with, a network of private-sector capacities and institutions. In several countries, this does not require the setting up of new institutions for capacity-building. Revamping the existing schools of public administration and enhancing their quality and prestige would go a long way to increasing capacity.

In most African countries, the private initiatives of independent research institutions do not attract much recognition or patronage from the government. Many of the indigenous R&D agencies depend almost exclusively on foreign foundations for their funding, so it is no surprise that most of the output is tailored to satisfying the particular interests of the donors. Beyond the regular funding of educational institutions, African governments need to take the issue of patronage for private-sector initiatives seriously.

Furthermore, the issue of capacity-building and the use of domestic capacity versus dependence on aid and technical assistance must be addressed. As mentioned earlier, SSA has about 100 000 foreign technical-assistance staff (advisers, consultants, etc.) costing about 4 billion USD per annum to maintain. In most cases, this staff substitutes for local capacity, but all current assessments of the impacts of this on SSA development are ostensibly negative. For example, Brautigam (1994, p. 94) provided startling statistics and recommended a strategy:

> Whether obtained through a grant or a loan, foreign expertise is not cheap: the annual cost can be up to $300,000 a year per expert. Housing, vehicles, and offices must be supplied, and salaries for foreign experts can be up to 100 times as high as [those for] their local counterparts, creating a situation ripe for resentment. In 1985, foreign experts resident in Equatorial Guinea were paid an amount nearly triple the total government public sector wage bill. Commonly, technical assistants introduce innovations that collapse after their departure.... . Strategies to build a more capable state will need to tackle the dependency created by foreign experts, while finding a way to tap the skills many of them possess.

The grants and loans that African countries receive should be used to build and sustain local capacity. Each country will have to devise strategies to resist taking grants tied to technical assistance unless a substantial part of that involves training of local staff (such as in staff exchange programs whereby local staff visit overseas institutions for skills training or overseas experts visit local institutions to provide training). A large portion of such grants could be channeled to fund special programs, such as in public-sector administration and policy analysis, in the universities and research institutes.

In much of current development thinking, the experiences of the East Asian tigers are touted as the new models of development. Unfortunately, many of the lessons from these development models come to Africans through intermediary channels, and African bureaucrats and their Asian counterparts scarcely interact to facilitate direct learning. An important initiative for African countries would be to actively cultivate some strategic relationships between their bureaucracies and those of the successful Asian economies. There can, in fact, be no better way of learning to create a developmental state and bureaucracy than through direct interaction with those who have the requisite experience.

Conclusions

Initial debates on adjustment were couched mainly in terms of whether the macroeconomic disequilibria were externally caused or induced by policy. This often gave the mistaken impression that national economies could be absolved from making the necessary adjustments. An important lesson from experience is that whatever the cause of the disequilibria, the burden of adjustment lies ultimately with the national economies, although complementary actions by the international community could greatly ease the cost of such adjustment. If, as African experience has shown, the expected external response is not forthcoming, individual countries have to carefully identify the structural and demand components of the disequilibria and choose an optimal mix of instruments to address the imbalances. African policymakers should take adjustment seriously. Adjustment in this sense entails a dynamic view of society and its capacity to continually adjust to changing domestic and external environments.

Perhaps the first important thing Africans can do is to reassume responsibility for plotting the paths of development in their respective countries. The tragedy of Africa's policy-making and policy implementation in the last several years is the complete surrender of national policies to the ever-changing ideas of international experts. Africans have lacked the confidence to consciously and vigorously craft and will a future for themselves. The first attempts that Africans made at articulating a framework for their development were in the Lagos Plan of Action, the Final Act of Lagos, and UNECA's African Alternative Framework to Structural Adjustment Programs. Most African governments signed the documents, and, to date, none of these governments has publicly dissociated itself from the ideas espoused in them. But the World Bank virulently attacked those documents, and every African government that wished to have successful debt rescheduling or aid negotiations distanced itself from the principles in them. What is not often appreciated is that most of what appears today as new insights about the imperatives of poverty reduction, investment in infrastructure and education, the requirements of rapid industrialization, and the structural and institutional bottlenecks of Africa's underdevelopment are nothing but the rehearsal of old but disparaged ideas of African scholars and policymakers.

If only Africans took themselves seriously and if only the international community listened, the long and costly learning curve could be minimized. The challenge is to blend macroeconomic stabilization cum adjustment under the SAPs with the detailed structural change and microeconomic and institutional transformations proposed by the Africans. The lessons from this costly experiment should provide the basis for future engagement.

For more than a decade, most of Africa has spent time and resources "adjusting" nonexistent or defective markets. It was hoped that getting the prices and the monetary or financial fundamentals right would be the one medicine needed to ensure the health of African economies: poverty reduction, equity, growth, industrialization, macrostability, and so forth. The plethora of micro and structural changes, the development of human capital and infrastructure, and the institution-building required for a modern capitalist economy were recognized only as important footnotes in the development model. Evidently, at least in most of SSA, the nostrums for all economic ills have been overwhelmed by the enormity of the ailment. The irony is that it has taken more than a decade for us to rediscover that, as the World Bank (1994, p. 2) finally admitted, "adjustment alone is not adequate for long-term sustainable development."

It has become commonplace to argue that measures adopted to deliberately accelerate development in other regions are inappropriate for Africa, not so much because things have changed but because of the alleged "peculiar" politics or culture of Africa. Our states are putatively more porous and vulnerable to capture than others. Our culture is not frugal enough or is downright antidevelopment. We invest too much in social relations to have any time for anything else. And on it goes. These views nourish the Afro-pessimistic stance that some have adopted. But they also nourish the arrogance of those who have chosen to assume the task of developing Africa without African involvement. As Ake (1991, p. 8) stressed, "the idea that a people or their culture and social institutions can be an obstacle to their development is one of the major confusions of current development thinking, and it is one of its most expensive errors." However, although we may loathe the attempts to locate Africa's poor performance on its supposedly immutable and peculiar characteristics, we must also recognize the need for fundamental changes in some of our attitudes, institutional arrangements, orientation to governance, and economic management. For example, the tensions and suspicion between the state and the capitalist class in many African countries that lead to massive capital outflows to safer havens are very unhealthy for the development of a capitalist economy. Furthermore, subordinating the national goals and development agenda to the narrow and often temporary interests of political survival or ethnic loyalty is hardly the best way to build a competitive and prosperous economy. In the end, there is no wishing away the sociopolitical issues that the transition to a market economy brings. Each country must, out of its own historical experiences, forge its own vision and design the requisite institutions to achieve development. Outsiders can assist, but this can never substitute for local initiative.

We cannot overstress the role that international conjuncture can play in widening or further narrowing the road ahead. Africa must learn to compete in this global arena. Such a learning process will be facilitated not just by developing and participating in regional markets but also by adopting an active strategy for increasing and diversifying Africa's exports. Africa's natural resources may facilitate this process, but we should recognize that only a strategy that relies on our human capacities will create a development process that can respond flexibly to circumstances in a rapidly changing world. Our natural-resource endowment will only contribute to development if we add intellectual value to it and if we use the revenue earned from it to transform and modernize agriculture and strengthen the development of an industrial sector made competitive by a strategically orchestrated exposure to competitiveness in international markets. The current wave of simply opening up more mines according to something akin to the colonial "enclave" model does not augur well for the use of natural resources for development.

Africa should know that it cannot integrate itself fully into the global economy by permanently depending on aid and preferential treatment. Neither of these has served Africa well. Aid has produced the phenomenon of the dependency syndrome that stifles both imagination and initiative, whereas preferential treatment (especially under the Lomé Convention) has provided incentives to perpetuate activities that fossilize our production structures in primary commodities. What Africa needs as it approaches the 21st century is not increased aid but a leveling of the playing field. An important element in this is an unconditional debt write-off for all the indebted SSA countries. Tying debt reduction to perceived compliance with certain performance standards may amount to circular reasoning. Poorly performing countries could blame their performance on the debt burden, whereas the high flyers may owe their growth to debt relief, which currently comes by way of increased official aid.

African economies are market economies. This means that although the state may draw up the larger developmental plans, implementing such plans depends on the responses of households, private entrepreneurs, and institutions. Two important lessons from Africa's development experience have been that failure to mobilize the resource-allocative functions of the market can only contribute to the inflexibility of the economy; and failure to recognize the weakness of market forces in a number of fundamental areas can lead to failed adjustment. Development policies will therefore have to be keenly responsive to the capacities and weaknesses of both states and markets in Africa and seek to mobilize the former while correcting the latter. Dogmatic faith in either planning or markets will simply not do.

Moving beyond adjustment to growth and development is, of course, not an easy task. The issues are complex, and a synthesis such as this cannot delve into all the issues. What emerges from the project is that Africa must take the driver's seat in moving the economies of the continent ahead. Africa must and can compete in a rapidly changing global environment. We must avoid a "failure complex," which leads to a tendency to adopt self-fulfilling blanket condemnations of our own reality and makes us incapable of learning from our experiences.

Moving African economies onto a development path will require robust state and societal institutions. These, in turn, will require creative mechanisms to produce a truly developmental state–society nexus able to synergistically mobilize human and physical resources and address the many contradictions inherent in our societies and in any processes of rapid change.

Economic development is quintessentially a political process involving the distribution of not only economic resources but also power. It is a process that taxes the political system heavily. It involves sacrifices and commitments that can only be sustained through a sense of shared vision and common purpose. It calls for the mobilization of national capacities. We have argued that such a process must be democratic, not only because of the inherent value of democracy but also because, given the nature of African societies — their social pluralism and the artificiality of national borders — and the current political conjuncture, only a democratic developmental state can acquire the adhesion of a citizenry as diverse as one finds in African countries.

Appendix

Abbreviations and Acronyms

ADB	African Development Bank
AERC	African Economic Research Consortium
BWI	Bretton Woods Institution
FDI	foreign direct investment
GDP	gross domestic product
GNP	gross national product
HIPC	highly indebted poor country
HPEA	high-performing East Asian economy
IFAD	International Fund for Agricultural Development
ILO	International Labor Organization
IMF	International Monetary Fund
ISI	import-substituting industrialization
MVA	manufacturing value added
NGO	nongovernmental organization
R&D	research and development
RORE	rate of return on education
S&T	science and technology
SAP	structural-adjustment program
SMEs	small- and medium-scale enterprises
SSA	sub-Saharan Africa
UNECA	United Nations Economic Commission for Africa

Bibliography

ADB (African Development Bank). 1994. African development report 1994. ADB, Abidjan, Côte d'Ivoire.

———— 1995. African development report 1995. ADB, Abidjan, Côte d'Ivoire.

Ahmed, R.; Rustagi, N. 1987. Marketing and price incentives in African and Asian countries: a comparison. In Elz, D., ed., Agricultural marketing strategies and pricing policy. World Bank, Washington, DC, USA.

Ake, C. 1979. Ideology and objective conditions. In Barkan, J.; Okumu, J., ed., Politics and public policy in Kenya and Tanzania. Heinneman, Nairobi, Kenya.

———— 1990. Democracy and development. West Africa, 26, 491.

———— 1991. Development on the indigenous. World Bank, Washington, DC, USA. Mimeo.

Ali, A.A.G. 1998. Structural adjustment and poverty in sub-Saharan Africa: 1985–1995. In Mkandawire, T.; Soludo, C.C., ed., African perspectives on structural adjustment, vol. 2. International Development Research Centre, Ottawa, ON, Canada. (In press.)

Amin, S. 1987. Democracy and the national strategy in the periphery. Third World Quarterly, 9(4), 1129–1156.

Anyang Nyong'o, P. 1988. Political instability and the prospects for democracy in Africa. Africa Development, 8(1), 71–86.

Appleton, S.; Mackinnon, J. 1996. Enhancing human capacities in Africa. In Ndulu, B.; van de Walle, N., ed., Agenda for Africa's economic renewal. Transaction Publishers, New Brunswick, NJ, USA. pp. 109–149.

Aron, J. 1996. The institutional foundations of growth. In Ellis, S., ed., Africa now: people, policies, institutions. James Currey, London, UK. pp. 93–118.

Auty, R. 1995. Economic development and the resource curse thesis. In Morissey, O.; Stewart, F., ed., Economic and political reform. St Martin's Press, New York, NY, USA.

Azzam, J.-P. 1996. The diversity of adjustment in agriculture. In Ellis, S., ed., Africa now: people, policies, institutions. James Currey, London, UK. pp. 136–154.

Bangura, Y. 1992. Authoritarian rule and democracy in Africa: a theoretical discourse. *In* Gibbon, P.; Bangura, Y.; Ofstad, A.E., ed., Authoritarianism, democracy and adjustment: the politics of economic reform in Africa. Scandinavian Institute of African Studies, Uppsala, Sweden. pp. 39–82.

Bayart, J.-F. 1993. The state in Africa: the politics of the belly. Longman, London, UK.

Bayoumi, T. 1990. Savings–investment correlations: immobile capital, government policy or endogenous behaviour. International Monetary Fund Papers, 37(2), 360–387.

Bennell, P. 1996. Rate of return to education: does the conventional pattern prevail in sub-Saharan Africa? World Development, 24(1), 183–199.

Bradford, C. 1994. The new paradigm of systemic competitiveness: why it matters, what it means and implications for policy. *In* Bradford, C., ed., The new paradigm of systemic competitiveness: toward more integrated policies in Latin America. Organization for Economic Co-operation and Development, Paris, France.

Brautigam, D. 1994. African industrialization in comparative perspective: the question of scale. *In* Berman, B.; Leys, C., ed., African capitalists in African development. Lynne Rienner, Boulder, CO, USA. pp. 139–159.

———— 1996. State capacity and effective governance. *In* Ndulu, B.; van de Walle, N., ed., Agenda for Africa's economic renewal. Transaction Publishers, New Brunswick, NJ, USA. pp. 81–108.

Bronfenbrenner, M. 1958. The appeal of confiscation in economic development. *In* Agarwala, A.N.; Singh, S.P., ed., The economics of underdevelopment. Oxford University Press, Oxford, UK.

Callaghy, T. 1990. Lost between state and market: the politics of economic adjustment in Ghana, Zambia and Nigeria. *In* Nelson, J., ed., Economic crisis and policy choice: the politics of adjustment in the Third World. Princeton University Press, Princeton, NJ, USA. pp. 257–320.

Chang, H. 1996. The political economy of industrial policy. Macmillan, London, UK.

Collier, P.; Gunning, J.W. 1997. Explaining African economic performance. Centre for the Study of African Economies, Oxford, UK.

Delgado, C. 1996. Agricultural transformation: the key to broad-based growth and poverty alleviation in Africa. *In* Ndulu, B.; van de Walle, N., ed., Agenda for Africa's economic renewal. Transaction Publishers, New Brunswick, NJ, USA. pp. 151–177.

Dell, S. 1982. Stabilization: the political economy of overkill. World Development, 10(8), 597–612.

Demery, L.; Squire, L. 1996. Macroeconomic adjustment and poverty in Africa. The World Bank Research Observer, 11(1).

Elbadawi, A.; Ndulu, B. 1996. Long-run development and sustainable growth in sub-Saharan Africa. In Lundhal, M.; Ndulu, B., ed., New directions in development economics: growth, environmental concerns and governments in the 1990s. Routledge, London, UK. pp. 323–351.

Elbadawi, I.; Ghura, D.; Uwujaren, G. 1992. Why structural adjustment has not succeeded in Africa. World Bank, Washington, DC, USA.

Elbadawi, I.A.; Uwujaren, G. 1992. World Bank adjustment lending and economic performance in sub-Saharan Africa in the 1980s. World Bank, Washington, DC, USA.

Elbadawi, I.A.; Ndulu, B.J.; Ndung'u, N. 1996. Debt overhang and economic growth in sub-Saharan Africa. In Conference on external financing for low-income countries. World Bank, Washington, DC, USA.

Engberg-Pedersen, P.; Gibbon, P.; Raikes, P.; Udholt, L., ed. 1996. Limits of adjustment in Africa. James Currey, London, UK.

Evans, P. 1992. The state as problem and solution: embedded autonomy, and structural change. In Haggard, S.A.; Kaufman, R., ed., The politics of economic adjustment: international constraints, distributive conflicts and the state. Princeton University Press, Princeton, NJ, USA. pp. 139–181.

Ewonkem, C. 1996. La réduction des coûts sociaux de l'ajustement structurel en afrique sub-saharienne. Paper presented at the Conference on African Perspectives on Structural Adjustment, 1996, Abidjan, Côte d'Ivoire. Council for the Development of Social Science Research in Africa, Dakar, Senegal.

Fanelli, J.M.; Frenkel, R. 1994. Macroeconomic policies for the transition from stabilisation to growth. In Bradford, C., ed., The new paradigm of systemic competitiveness: toward more integrated policies in Latin America. Organization for Economic Co-operation and Development, Paris, France. pp. 209–227.

Feldstein, M.; Horioka, C. 1980. Domestic savings and international capital flows. Economic Journal, 90(358), 314–329.

Felix, D. 1994. Industrial development in East Asia: what are the lessons for Latin America. United Nations Conference on Trade and Development, Geneva, Switzerland.

Fernandez, A. 1993. Stabilisation, exports and regional development: the Northeast in the 1980s. University of Sussex, Brighton, UK. Research Paper No. 8.

Giovanni, A. 1983. The interest elasticity of savings in developing countries: the existing evidence. World Development, 11(7), 601–607.

Greenwald, B.; Stigliz J.E. 1984. Informational imperfections in capital markets and macroeconomic fluctuations. American Economic Review, 74, 194–199.

———— 1986. Externalities in economies with imperfect information and incomplete markets. Quarterly Journal of Economics, 101, 229–264.

Griffin, K. 1996. Macroeconomic reform and employment: an investment-led strategy of structural adjustment in sub-Saharan Africa. International Labour Office, Geneva, Switzerland.

Gyimah-Boadi, E.; van de Walle, N. 1996. The politics of economic renewal in Africa. In Ndulu, B.; van de Walle, N., ed., Agenda for Africa's economic renewal. Transaction Publishers, New Brunswick, NJ, USA.

Helleiner, G. 1994. From adjustment to development in sub-Saharan Africa: consensus and continuing conflict. In Cornia, G.; Helleiner, G., ed., From adjustment to development in Africa: conflict, controversy, convergence, consensus? Macmillan, London, UK. pp. 3–24.

Helpman, E.; Krugman, P. 1985. Market structure and foreign trade: increasing returns, imperfect competition and the international economy. Massachusetts Institute of Technology Press, Cambridge, MA, USA.

Hurwicz, L. 1995. Social absorption capability and economic development. In Hoo, B.H., ed., Social capability and long-term economic growth. Macmillan, London, UK.

Hussain, I. 1994. Structural development and the long-term development of sub-Saharan Africa. In van der Hoeven, R.; van der Kraaj, F., ed., Structural adjustment and beyond in sub-Saharan Africa. James Currey, London, UK. pp. 150–172.

Hussain, I.; Faruqee, R., ed. 1994. Adjustment in Africa: lessons from country case studies. World Bank, Washington, DC, USA.

Hutchful, E. 1995. Adjustment in Africa and fifty years of the Bretton Woods institutions: change or consolidation. Canadian Journal of Development Studies, 16(3), 391–417.

ILO (International Labor Organization). 1996. World employment 1996/97: national policies in a global context. ILO, Geneva, Switzerland.

IMF (International Monetary Fund). 1997. World economic outlook. IMF, Washington, DC, USA.

Inanga, E.L.; Ekpenyong, D.B. 1998. Financial liberalization in Africa: legal and institutional framework and lessons from other developing countries. In Mkandawire, T.; Soludo, C.C., ed., African perspectives on structural adjustment, vol. 2. International Development Research Centre, Ottawa, ON, Canada. (In press.)

Jaycox, E.V.K. 1993. Capacity building: the missing link in African development. Address to the African-American Institute, 20 May 1993, Reston, VA, USA. African-American Institute, Washington, DC, USA.

Johnson, H. 1967. A theoretical model of economic nationalism in new and developing countries. *In* Johnston, H.G., ed., Economic nationalism in old and new states. University of Chicago Press, Chicago, IL, USA.

Killick, T. 1992. Just how important is finance for African development. *In* Patel, I.G., ed., Policies for African development: from the 1980s to the 1990s. International Monetary Fund, Washington, DC, USA.

——— ed. 1995. The flexible economy: causes, consequences of the adaptability of national economies. Routledge, London, UK.

——— 1996. Principals, agents and the limitations of BWI conditionality. World Economy, 19(2).

Krugman, P. 1992. Toward a counter-counterrevolution in development theory. *In* Proceedings of the World Bank Annual Conference on Development Economics. World Bank Economic Review (suppl.), 15–39.

Lal, D. 1996. Participation, markets and democracy. *In* Lundahl, M.; Ndelu, B.J., ed., New directions in development economics. Routledge, London, UK. pp. 229–322.

Lall, S. 1995. Structural adjustment and African industry. World Development, 23(12).

Lall, S.; Stewart, F. 1996. Trade and industrial policy in Africa. *In* Ndulu, B.; van de Walle, N., ed., Agenda for Africa's economic renewal. Transaction Publications, New Brunswick, NJ, USA. pp. 179–209.

Lancaster, C. 1991. African economic reform: the external dimension. Institute for International Economics, Washington, DC, USA.

Mamdani, M. 1995. Democratic theory and democratic struggles. *In* Chole, E.; Ibrahim, J., ed., Democratisation processes in Africa: problems and prospects. Council for the Development of Social Science Research in Africa, Dakar, Senegal. pp. 43–80.

McKinnon, R. 1973. Money and capital in economic development. The Brookings Institution, Washington, DC, USA. 184 pp.

Mkandawire, T. 1988. The road to crisis, adjustment and de-industrialization: the African case. Africa Development, 13(1), 5–32.

——— 1995. Fiscal structure, state contraction and political responses in Africa. *In* Mkandawire, T.; Adebayo, O., ed., Between liberalisation and repression: the politics of adjustment in Africa. Council for the Development of Social Science Research in Africa, Dakar, Senegal. pp. 20–51.

——— 1996. Economic policy-making and the consolidation of democratic institutions in Africa. *In* Havnevik, K.; van Arkadie, B., ed., Domination or dialogue: experiences and prospects for Africa development co-operation. Nordiska Afrikainstitutet, Uppsala, Sweden.

Mosley, P. 1996. Globalisation, economic policy and poverty in sub-Saharan Africa, 1970–95. Department of Economics, University of Reading, Reading, UK.

Mwega, F.M. 1998. Financial sector reform in Eastern and Southern Africa. In Mkandawire, T.; Soludo, C.C., ed., African perspectives on structural adjustment, vol. 2. International Development Research Centre, Ottawa, ON, Canada. (In press.)

Mwega, F.M., Ngola, S.M.; Mwangi, N. 1992. Real interest rates and the mobilisation of private savings in Africa. African Economic Research Consortium, Nairobi, Kenya.

Myrdal, G. 1957. Economic nationalism and internationalism. Australian Institute of International Affairs, Melbourne, Australia.

Nissanke, M. 1994. Financial policies and intermediation performance. In van der Geest, W., ed., Negotiating structural adjustment in Africa. James Currey, London, UK. pp. 161–174.

———— 1997. Africa: institutions, policies and development. International Development Center of Japan, Tokyo, Japan.

Ogwumike, F. 1998. Structural adjustment and poverty in Africa. In Conference on African perspectives on structural adjustment. Council for the Development of Social Science Research in Africa, Abidjan, Côte d'Ivoire.

Olukoshi, A. 1998. The elusive Prince of Denmark: structural adjustment and the crisis of governance in Africa. In Conference on African perspectives on structural adjustment. Council for the Development of Social Science Research in Africa, Abidjan, Côte d'Ivoire.

Olukoshi, A.O.; Laakso, L., ed. 1996. Changes to the nation-state in Africa. Nordiska Afrikainstitutet, Uppsala, Sweden. 213 pp.

Opio, F. 1996. Structural adjustment, growth and poverty in Uganda. Economic Policy Research Centre, Kampala, Uganda. EPRC Bulletin.

Oshikoya, T.W.; Ogbu, O. 1998. Financial liberalization, emerging stock markets, and economic development in Africa. In Mkandawire, T.; Soludo, C.C., ed., African perspectives on structural adjustment, vol. 2. International Development Research Centre, Ottawa, ON, Canada. (In press.)

Oyejide, T.A. 1996. Regional integration and trade liberalisation in sub-Saharan Africa: summary report. Macmillan, London, UK.

———— 1998. Trade liberalization, regional integration, and African development in the context of structural adjustment. In Mkandawire, T.; Soludo, C.C., ed., African perspectives on structural adjustment, vol. 2. International Development Research Centre, Ottawa, ON, Canada. (In press.)

Park, Y.C. 1993. The role of finance in economic development in South Korea and Taiwan. *In* Giovannini, A., ed., Finance and development: issues and experience. Cambridge University Press, Cambridge, UK. pp. 121–157.

Rodrik, D. 1995. Trade and industrial policies. *In* Berman, J.; Strinivasan, T.N., ed., Handbook of development economics. Elsevier Scientific, Amsterdam, Netherlands.

Sachs, J. 1996. Growth in Africa: it can be done. The Economist, 1996 (June 29), 19–21.

——— 1997. The limits of convergence: nature, nurture and growth. The Economist, 1997 (June 14).

Sachs, J.D.; Warner, M. 1995. Natural resources and economic growth. Harvard Institute for International Development, Cambridge, MA, USA.

——— 1996. Sources of slow growth in African economies. Harvard Institute for International Development, Cambridge, MA, USA.

Schatzenberg, M. 1980. The state and the economy: the radicalisation of the revolution in Mobutu's Zaire. Canadian Journal of African Studies, 14.

Schiavo-Campo, S. 1996. Reforming the civil service. Finance and Development, 33(3), 10–13.

Shaffer, D.M. 1994. Winners and losers: how sectors shape the developmental prospects of states. Cornell University, Ithaca, NY, USA.

Shivji, I. 1980. The state in the dominated social formations of Africa: some theoretical issues. International Social Science Journal, 32, 4.

Singh, A. 1995. The causes of fast economic growth in East Asia. United Nations Conference on Trade and Development, Geneva, Switzerland.

Soludo, C.C. 1993. Growth performance in Africa: further evidence on the external shocks versus domestic policy debate. United Nations Economic Commission for Africa, Addis Ababa, Ethiopia.

——— 1997. Between free trade and mercantilism: Africa's choice of trade and industrial policies. Council for the Development of Social Science Research in Africa, Dakar, Senegal.

——— 1998. Industrialization and growth in sub-Saharan Africa: is the Asian experience useful? *In* Mkandawire, T.; Soludo, C.C., ed., African perspectives on structural adjustment, vol. 2. International Development Research Centre, Ottawa, ON, Canada. (In press.)

Ssemogerere, G. 1998. Financial sector restructuring under the SAPs and economic development. *In* Mkandawire, T.; Soludo, C.C., ed., African perspectives on structural adjustment, vol. 2. International Development Research Centre, Ottawa, ON, Canada. (In press.)

Stewart, F. 1995. Adjustment and poverty: options and choices. Routledge, London, UK.

Stiglitz, J. 1989. Markets, market failures, and development. American Economic Review, 79(3), 197–203.

———— 1993. The role of the state in financial markets. In Proceedings of the World Bank Annual Conference on Development Economics. World Bank Economic Review (suppl.), 19–52.

Stiglitz, J.; Uy, M. 1996. Financial markets, public policy, and East Asian miracle. World Bank Research Observer, 11(2), 249–276.

Taylor, L. 1983. Structuralist macroeconomics. Basic Books, New York, NY, USA.

Tendler, J. 1997. Good government in the tropics. Johns Hopkins University Press, Baltimore, MD, USA.

Toye, J. 1994. Structural adjustment: context, assumptions, origin and diversity. In Hoeven, R.V.D.; Kraaij, F.V.D., ed., Structural adjustment and beyond in sub-Saharan Africa. Ministry of Foreign Affairs, Government of the Netherlands, The Hague, Netherlands.

Tshibaka, T. 1996. Structural adjustment, agricultural output and income in sub-Saharan Africa. In Mkandawire, T.; Soludo, C.C., ed., African perspectives on structural adjustment, vol. 2. International Development Research Centre, Ottawa, ON, Canada (In press.)

UNCTAD (United Nations Conference on Trade and Development). 1995. Foreign direct investment in Africa — 1995. UNCTAD, Geneva, Switzerland.

———— 1996. UNCTAD Secretariat report to the conference on East Asian development: lessons for a new global environment. UNCTAD, Geneva, Switzerland.

Vivian, J. 1995. Adjustment and social sector restructuring. Journal of Development Research, 7, 11.

Wangwe, S.M., ed. 1995. Exporting Africa: technology, trade and industrialization in sub-Saharan Africa. Routledge, London, UK.

Wangwe, S.M.; Semboja, H.H. 1998. Impact of structural adjustment on industrialization and technology in Africa. In Mkandawire, T.; Soludo, C.C., ed., African perspectives on structural adjustment, vol. 2. International Development Research Centre, Ottawa, ON, Canada. (In press.)

Wellons, P.A. 1977. Borrowing by developing countries on the Euro-currency market. Organization for Economic Co-operation and Development, Paris, France.

Wheeler, D. 1994. Sources of stagnation in sub-Saharan Africa. World Development, 12(1), 1–23.

World Bank. 1981. Accelerated development for Africa: an agenda for Africa. World Bank, Washington, DC, USA.

————— 1988. Education in sub-Saharan Africa: policies of adjustment, revitalisation, and expansion. World Bank, Washington, DC, USA.

————— 1989a. Africa's adjustment and growth in the 1980s. World Bank, Washington, DC, USA.

————— 1989b. Sub-Saharan Africa: from crisis to sustainable growth. World Bank, Washington, DC, USA.

————— 1990. Adjustment lending policies for sustainable growth. World Bank, Washington, DC, USA.

————— 1993. The East Asian miracle: economic growth and public policy. World Bank, Washington, DC, USA.

————— 1994. Adjustment in Africa: reforms, results and the road ahead. World Bank, Washington, DC, USA.

————— 1995. A continent in transition: sub-Saharan Africa in the mid-1990s. World Bank, Washington, DC, USA. Draft.

————— 1996. Structural aspects of manufacturing in sub-Saharan Africa: findings from a seven country enterprise survey. World Bank, Washington, DC, USA.

————— 1997. World development report 1997. World Bank, Washington, DC, USA.

Young, C. 1982. Ideology and development in Africa. Yale University Press, New Haven, CT, USA.

————— 1994. Lessons from the East Asia NICs: a contrarian view. European Economic Review, 38(3/4).

Index

f indicates page following; ff indicates two pages following; t indicates table

The Publishers

The International Development Research Centre (IDRC) is committed to building a sustainable and equitable world. IDRC funds developing-world researchers, thus enabling the people of the South to find their own solutions to their own problems. IDRC also maintains information networks and forges linkages that allow Canadians and their developing-world partners to benefit equally from a global sharing of knowledge. Through its actions, IDRC is helping others to help themselves. IDRC Books publishes research results and scholarly studies on global and regional issues related to sustainable and equitable development. As a specialist in development literature, IDRC Books contributes to the body of knowledge on these issues to further the cause of global understanding and equity. IDRC publications are sold through its head office in Ottawa, Canada, as well as by IDRC's agents and distributors around the world.

CODESRIA is the Council for the Development of Social Science Research in Africa headquartered in Senegal. It is an independent organization whose principal objectives are facilitating research, promoting research-based publishing and creating multiple forums geared towards the exhange of views and information among African researchers. It challenges the fragmentation of research through the creation of thematic research networks that cut across linguistic and regional boundaries. CODESIRA publishes a quarterly journal, *Africa Development*, the longest-standing Africa-based journal, *African Sociological Review*, *Afrika Zamani* and *African Journal of International Affairs*. Research results are disseminated through Working Papers, The Monograph Series, and The CODESRIA Book Series.

Africa World Press (AWP) and The Red Sea Press (RSP) are "sister presses" based in Lawrenceville, New Jersey, and dedicated to the publication and distribution of books on the African world. In a period in which the publishing industry in the United States is undergoing dramatic changes, these publishing houses are fulfilling a great demand for "non-mainstream" academic texts, poetry, short stories and children's books. Unlike other small and medium-sized presses, which often publish only a handful of books each year, AWP and RSP are dedicated to the publication of as many books as is feasible. Other publishers often let Third World books go quickly out of print. Our catalogue includes a number of books that are new editions of out-of-print books or US editions of books originally published in other countries — both hard-to-find categories we know our readers are eager to read.